Seein

Seeing Ourselves

Interpreting Contemporary Society

Libby Purves, Robert Blake,
Danah Zohar & John Habgood

edited and introduced by Stephen Platten
with an afterword by Elizabeth Estéve-Coll

CANTERBURY
PRESS
Norwich

First published in 1998 by The Canterbury Press Norwich
(a publishing imprint of Hymns Ancient & Modern Limited
a registered charity)
St Mary's Works, St Mary's Plain
Norwich, Norfolk, NR3 3BH

British Library Cataloguing in Publication Data

A catalogue record for this book is available
from the British Library

ISBN 1-85311-231-3

Typeset by Rowland Phototypesetting,
Bury St Edmunds, Suffolk
Printed in Great Britain by
Biddles Ltd, Guildford and King's Lynn

Contents

Preface

In the second half of the twentieth century, on occasions there has prevailed a mutual suspicion between the Church and the secular institutions responsible for education. The roots of such suspicion are not difficult to uncover: an over-clericalized Church has often threatened the autonomy of schools and universities, the process referred to as 'secularization' calls into question the existence of the churches, and even the legitimacy of theological study has been called into doubt by some forms of positivist philosophy. At root, questions of truth and the pursuit of truth have been there even if they have not been acknowledged as such.

The period following the Robbins Report and the establishment of new universities in Britain coincided with a strong recurrence of that suspicion. The foundation of the University of East Anglia (UEA) was no exception to this and its charter rules out the teaching of confessional theology. From the beginning, however, there were those who were committed to dialogue and conversation which reached out beyond the walls of suspicion. The first Vice-Chancellor of UEA, Professor Frank Thistlethwaite, focused such a commitment from the University's point of view. From the churches, undoubtedly the key figure was Bishop Launcelot

Fleming, Bishop of Norwich from 1959 to 1971. Fleming's whole being manifested a desire for religion and the secular, Christianity and the life of the nation, to be in conversation with each other. As the memoire which follows indicates, his own life had mirrored such experience.

When it was decided by the University and the Cathedral in Norwich to establish a series of lectures, Launcelot Fleming was the obvious person whose name should be honoured. There are many to whom we are indebted in the setting up of these lectures. First there is Jane Fleming, Launcelot's widow, who enthusiastically embraced the suggestion that the lectures should bear his name. Second, at the university, Elizabeth Estéve-Coll gave great personal commitment. Without her help, and both the intellectual and practical assistance of Professor Colin Davis, the setting up of the series would have been impossible.

Within this book are included the 1997 lectures, an introduction, and a memoire of Launcelot Fleming in the form of the sermon preached in the Cathedral at the service for the dedication of the plaque in his memory on the 4th February 1996.

Stephen Platten
Norwich
February 1998

A Note on Launcelot Fleming

*'O ye holy and humble men of heart, bless ye
the Lord . . .'*

Those opening words of the Benedicite seem very apt
for Launcelot Fleming. The Benedicite is a great poem
of praise to God. Man blessing God for all his works
in creation. The beauty and grandeur of the natural
world meant much to Launcelot. He was trained in science and became a geologist. He would be interested to
think that his memorial in Norwich Cathedral is made
of Portland stone. My hope in the first instance was
that we could find stone or slate from Scotland – his
birthplace – but that trail went dead. However, I think
that he would be happy with the final choice – Portland
has naval connections and links in with happy years of
retirement spent in Dorset.

Launcelot was the youngest of five children. The
youngest child always has a special place in any family.
His parents had a portrait painted of him when he was
seven, a splendid and charming picture. In it you can
see the quiet determination that was such a key part of
his character. Two of his mother's brothers were
ordained in the Church of England. His father – he often
liked to quote this – was an elder of the kirk. One of
the uncles, Bishop Holland, became Dean of Norwich.
After school Launcelot went up to Cambridge to read

natural sciences. His college was Trinity Hall and it has been said that he was never quite rational about the Hall. He served the college as Chaplain and Dean and kept close links with the place until he died.

It was during his time as Chaplain that he went to the Antarctic. This expedition was truly a journey of exploration. They went by sailing ship and were away from home for three years. It was the first major British expedition to go after Captain Scott. It was an epic pioneering exploration and their work was dangerous. The long expedition required much courage and great physical stamina. Launcelot went as a geologist, but also as Chaplain, friend and adviser to all on board. The words 'Antarctic explorer' are rightly on his memorial, but it must be said that Launcelot was not only an explorer of ice and snow and rocks, but also an explorer of *truth*. He always valued his service as a wartime Chaplain in the Royal Navy. At the end of the war he was given the job of helping to select service candidates who were offering for the ordained ministry. Here, all his pastoral gifts came into play. He had an uncanny knack of getting alongside young people. Indeed, he must have fostered and encouraged more vocations than almost anyone in the Church of England. He was for ever telling anyone he saw, 'You ought to consider being ordained.'

Although a shy and self-effacing man, Launcelot was greatly endowed with pastoral gifts and the gift of friendship. It was very quickly clear that of all the epithets suggested, those of *pastor* and *friend* came most readily to mind. A Bishop is a pastor, pastor to the whole diocese and especially *pastor pastorum*. Launcelot's *friends* were legion – many people have written about his memorial and told of the ways that he influenced their life. He kept in touch with so many, but at the heart of it all he was a friend of Christ. His care for others all stemmed from his faith.

The memorial is set in the cathedral because he was Bishop of Norwich. When he was appointed it was a happy connection that his old college, Trinity Hall, had been founded by Bishop Bateman, Bishop of Norwich in 1350, at the height of the Black Death. And what of his ministry at Norwich? He had a great care and concern for the clergy and their families. He insisted that clergy chapters should meet – those were the days of clerical societies. He set up the Calendar of Intercession. He organized a Summer School at Keswick Hall. He worked to set up groups and team ministries in the countryside. He was a great friend of the young; there were four youth Chaplains in the diocese. He appointed a Chaplain at Anglia TV. He set up the Brooke Report for the city of Norwich. He worked tirelessly as a member of the Council at UEA and made an outstanding contribution. He came to it as a don, a scientist and not an arts man and this was an advantage. The Chaplaincy was set up and its building was created through his efforts. And perhaps mention should be made of the Bishop's hockey XI. Sport and games were an essential part of Launcelot's life: tennis, squash, rowing, hockey, swimming, walking and climbing in the Highlands. He was a keen competitor and loved to take exercise. He had a wry and subtle sense of humour, a good sense of timing in telling stories and *above all* the capacity to laugh at himself.

He once said that one of the best series of talks that he ever gave was to a conference of dons and beaks in the early 1950s. The titles of the addresses give a clue to the virtues that he most admired – humility, compassion and courage. I suppose that the letters on his memorial which are least well known are FRSE: Fellow of the Royal Society of Edinburgh. They are there to speak of his roots in Scotland and his science. It so happened that as I was preparing this word, those letters kept recurring: F – Friend, Father in God; R – Royalty and Rowing (in 1949 he helped to coach the Boat Race crew); S – Science, Students and Squash; E – Edinburgh, Energy and Exploration. The compass points at the foot of the stone have a cross at their centre. Here is the heart of our faith but also the globe shows a man with a world vision. He was an explorer – of rocks and of truth.

Environmental issues were close to his heart in the days before they become fashionable. In 1970 he became a member of the Royal Commission on Environmental Pollution. During his time in Norwich he spoke in the House of Lords on various subjects – leisure, family life, university education, factory farming, international control of the seabed and, in 1967, he piloted the Antarctic Treaty Conservation bill through the House of Lords. He was a Bishop not afraid to play on a wider stage. Launcelot was gentle, charming, full of tact and courtesy – but with a centre of steel. He was very determined and had a shrewd and canny sense of getting what he wanted. I remember him with thankfulness, with love and with great affection. Thucydides has a wonderful sentence in the funeral ovation, 'the burial place of noble men is in the hearts of their friends'.

'*O ye holy and humble men of heart, bless ye the Lord . . .*'

Richard Hanmer[1]

Note

1. Sermon preached at Evensong on Sunday 4th February 1996 before the dedication of the Memorial Plaque to Bishop Launcelot Fleming.

Introduction

'The revolutions of 1989–91 brought about the end of the order ushered in by the Kaiser's war, and greatly reinforced by Hitler's war: a revolutionary Russia, the new nation-states packaged up at Versailles, the growth of Soviet power, the terminal weakening of Britain and France, the division of Europe into two mutually hostile camps, each dominated by a super-power. As the smoke begins to clear, the landscape looks very different. Russia is exhausted, America is in retreat, Western Europe assuming something of its pre-1914 importance. A more traditional form of diplomacy is springing up, free of the great post-war ideological blocks.'[1]

That fascinating analysis of international politics with its interpretative pointers for the future comes not from the pen of a professional historian, nor indeed from the reflections of a student of political science. Instead it is an interpretation of events offered by a television journalist. From that point of view it is a new phenomenon mirroring the culture of a so-called post-modern world. As a piece of interpretation, however, it stands within a tradition that extends all the way back to the roots of western culture in ancient Greece. Intelligent commentators, whatever their own intellectual background, have never been frightened of offering an interpretation of the past alongside advice for ordering the future. Prota-goras' famous utterance – 'Man is the measure of all things' – sums up this confidence in our human ability to transcend the world in which we are placed. We do not, however, have to agree with the implied relativism of Protagoras' insight while accepting his general point about humanity's capacity for self-reflection.

Within the corpus of ancient Greek philosophy, prob-ably the two most significant analyses of social relation-ships within society are those of Plato in his *Republic* and of Aristotle in his *Politics*. Even Aristotle's famous observation that 'man is a political animal' is but the beginning of a wider interpretation. In *The Republic* Plato attempts a famous – indeed in the eyes of Karl Popper and others a notorious – analysis of the elements which must be included to fashion a prosperous and well-ordered society. His categorization of humanity into men of brass, iron, wood etc. and his advocacy of the censorship of literature and music are seen by Popper as a recipe for totalitarianism. Interpretation of society with an eye to forming the future is no new feature of the human landscape, nor are contemporary attempts to do this more controversial than those of earlier ages, as the case of Plato indicates.

The advent of the Christian era added a different set of ingredients into the culture which comprised the world of mid-antiquity. The period including the ministry of Jesus and the subsequent sub-apostolic world was one of tumult and uncertainty. The Near East had been a region of instability and conflict for many centuries.

This experience of instability, standing alongside the contributions from contemporary religious traditions, resulted in the growth of eschatological and apocalyptic patterns of thought. In other words, building upon contemporary Jewish thought and Zoroastrian beliefs from Persia, the teaching and ministry of Jesus, and indeed its interpretation within the early Church, assumed the possibility that the 'end of all things' was coming upon the world. God would break in and wind up the universe with terrifying signs accompanying this. Such thinking is well exemplified in the Revelation to St John the Divine and also in the 'little apocalypses' of the first three 'synoptic' gospels. The account in Mark's gospel puts it thus:

> But in those days, after that tribulation, the sun will be darkened, and the moon will not give its light, and the stars will be falling from heaven, and the powers in the heavens will be shaken. And then they will see the Son of Man coming in clouds with great power and glory. And then he will send out the angels, and gather his elect from the four winds, from the ends of the earth to the ends of heaven.[2]

This vivid language mirrored the instability of the times and it brought with it the belief that such instability must pre-figure the intervention by God in his world. This particular saying of Jesus was interpreted alongside others to mean that Jesus himself would come again to wind up all things and complete the establishment of the 'kingdom of God'. Society was interpreted using a theological critique which was itself fashioned by both history and religious experience. It did not take long for this innovative method of interpretation to be revised in the light of experience. Even within the compass of the New Testament one encounters a later and less apocalyptic strand where the kingdom of God is seen as having been established already in the coming of Jesus Christ. New Testament theologians have called this 'realized eschatology'. This feeling is powerful in the Gospel of John. It is there too, on occasions, in the writings of Paul. At one point Paul declares:

> Now these things happened to them as a warning, but they were written down for our instruction, upon whom the end of the ages has come.[3]

Paul is reinterpreting the more terrifying moments within recent history and experience differently. Now, it appears, the reign or kingdom of God has already arrived. Obviously both sorts of interpretation could have a significant impact upon the way people live their lives. The tiny 'sectarian' Christian community was fashioned on one of two sets of assumptions. Either God was about to break in and ethics and relations with wider society would exist only for the interim; or the kingdom was already here and Christians must live according to the principles expected by God as part of his reign within humanity. In either case, Christians were a tiny minority and the more important interpretations for wider society were those included within the *Pax Romana*. With the collapse of the Greek Empire, much of that earlier culture had been subsumed within the newer Roman Empire and a burgeoning Latin culture emerged. The spread of Christianity was slow and patchy in the first three centuries and it was related to the effectiveness of rival gods in supporting prosperity and victory in war.[4] It was the conversion of Constantine in AD 312, when he fought under the sign of the cross and was victorious at the battle of Milvian Bridge, that transformed the situation in late antiquity. In the following year, Constantine proclaimed a policy of religious freedom and favour to Christianity. Despite future imperial apostasy and the vicissitudes of Christianity under later emperors, this heralded the establishment of the polity of Christendom in medieval Europe.

The triumph of a Christian interpretation of human destiny and of society is pre-figured in Constantine's construction of the great basilicas of Hagia Sophia in Constantinople (formerly Byzantium and now the 'new Rome'), of the Holy Sepulchre in Jerusalem and of the Nativity in Bethlehem. In the Church of the Nativity one can still see fragments of the mosaics fashioned for Constantine's original basilica of AD 325. This basilican pattern of an oblong hall with an apsidal end was itself taken from the secular building of this period of late antiquity. The Aula Palatina in Trier in Germany is an example of a secular building taken over by the Christian Church as a place of worship. Instead of the Roman prefect sitting at the centre of the apse, the bishop had usurped his position. Here then lay also the roots of Romanesque architecture, which would also form the seedbed for the later development of Gothic architecture in western Europe and, in a very different manner, of the neo-classical of the Renaissance period.

This synthesis of Christianity and Christian interpretation with the earlier cultural tradition soon spread to the west. It is most perfectly seen, perhaps, in the life and influence of Gregory the Great, Pope from 590 to 604. Gregory came from an aristocratic family; he was the son of a Roman senator and was prefect of the city from 573. Later, he sold his property and set up monasteries (over one of which he himself became the abbot). It was from this same monastery that Gregory would send Augustine, his prior, to take the gospel back to the Kentish shores of Britain to convert the heathen Angles. Gregory, who was perhaps the single most important architect of the medieval papacy, ruled over a Church which was characterized by a network of urban dioceses throughout Latin Europe. It was this model that was the intellectual foundation of Bede's ecclesiastical history of England, even though in his heart and affections Bede had much sympathy with some of the spiritual traditions of the Irish Celtic church.

Bede's remarkable history once again assumes an integrated interpretation of society from within a Christian framework.[5] The assumptions are still early medieval with the powerful hold of miracle; the earlier New Testament patterns of apocalyptic eschatology have not been abandoned entirely. But there is now also a clear and Constantinian relationship between the secular powers and the religious establishment, even if, at times, the relationship is stormy. Indeed, it was Oswald, King of the Northumbrians, who would invite the Irish monks on Iona to send a missionary bishop to his kingdom; Aidan's arrival at Lindisfarne marked the beginning of a tradition of bishops advising kings. Lindisfarne was close to the royal palace at Bamburgh and Bede notes:

> The King always listened humbly and readily to Aidan's advice and diligently set himself to establish and extend the Church of Christ throughout his kingdom.[6]

Elsewhere, Bede records similar advice to Oswald's successor, Oswin.

In England, this confluence of the secular and the religious is clear again in the culture that prevailed, following the Norman conquest. Key cities were identified to subdue and govern the surrounding regions. Essential to this process was the policy of moving cathedrals, as the seats of bishops, from less prominent rural centres to key regional cities. In East Anglia, the see city moved from Thetford (only a fairly brief resting place – it had been at North Elmham for at least two centuries) to Norwich. In 1072, Bishop Remigius had moved his cathedral from Dorchester-on-Thames to Lincoln. The Christian structures remained a powerful element within the patterns that interpreted and thus governed Norman society. The Romanesque architecture of the earlier Roman Empire came with these Scandinavian/French conquerors.

This pattern did not always result in harmony. Anselm, one of the great intellectual imports into England following the Norman invasion, found himself in almost constant conflict with William II, his sovereign. Issues of jurisdiction resulted in exile for Anselm and an appeal to the Pope. Similar issues fuelled the celebrated and tragic dispute between Henry II and Thomas Becket. Finally, it would be political issues that would play a most significant part in the patterns of English Reformation in the sixteenth century. England was not alone in experiencing such conflict and controversy.

This confluence and sometimes conflict was, however, not only increasingly significant in its effects in the corridors of power. It had an effect upon the intellectual tradition, too. The cross-fertilization of Greek thought with that of the Christian tradition became an essential part of this pattern with the work of Thomas Aquinas in the thirteenth century. Aquinas' systematization of Christian theology using Aristotelian categories further helped theology become the 'queen of the sciences' and thus an essential tool in the interpretation of human experience within medieval society. But this process of intellectual development was as important because of its personnel as it was in terms of the development of western thought and the history of ideas. Knowledge was almost entirely the possession of a clerical élite. The growth of the universities in Europe was dependent upon the monasteries. This is still obvious in the architectural patterns seen in Oxford and Cambridge colleges. Indeed, until the last century one could not be a Fellow of a college within the ancient universities without also being a priest of the Church of England. Even on official documents today, I am still bidden to style myself '*Clerk* in Holy Orders'.

Introduction

It was not only the growth of knowledge, then, but also its diffusion and control that lay within the hands of the Church. Ecclesiastical influence and authority could be terrifying in their power. The stories of Giordano Bruno and Galileo Galilei are perhaps the most celebrated examples of the 'new knowledge' coming into conflict with the magisterium of the Church. Christian theology not only interpreted human experience, but it did so within strict canons of authority. It was the Christian tradition, or rather the Christian tradition as understood by the senior authorities within the Church, that decided whether the earth was round or flat, and whether the sun orbited the earth or vice versa.

The Reformation within western Europe would shatter many of these patterns and effectively fragment Christendom. In itself, it may be that the Reformation was the single most significant contributor to that process that would eventually inhibit theology from being the key interpreter of human society. The politics of the Reformation within western European nation states are a complex and fascinating study. Kings, princes and governors were keen to preserve their power and sever some of the key links with the 'Bishop of Rome'. Even within the Reformation, however, clerical and theological influence within society remained seminal. Thomas Cranmer cut his teeth, as an ecclesiastical statesman and fashioner of a new secular and religious polity, in the tough and Machiavellian world of international diplomacy. He was effectively an ambassador (or at least a First Secretary!) for Henry VIII in missions to both Spain and Italy, and later to Central Europe. The settlement which emerged before Cranmer's fall from power under Mary Tudor, was a settlement rooted in the Royal Supremacy which still held together secular and ecclesiastical polity. This polity was further refined in the Elizabethan settlement. Richard Hooker's book *Laws of Ecclesiastical Polity* is, amongst other things, an attempt to make sense of this new world and to offer a flexible model that would allow for development in the future.

It was not only the Reformation, of course, that prefigured cultural and intellectual shifts in European society. Enlightenment thought and the growth of modern science both contributed important elements to these changes. In England, many of the key enlightenment figures remained believers but their belief would often be characterized by a broad deism, which is readily identifiable in the thought of both Isaac Newton and John Locke. Furthermore, philosophical development during this period marked the end of the enduring Aristotelian consensus; philosophical thought could no longer be understood as developmental and additive, as Alasdair MacIntyre has demonstrated with such eloquence.[7] Nevertheless, it was not really until the mid-nineteenth century that all of this came home to roost.

As the nineteenth century wore on, an increasing secularization of education emerged in England. This shift began with the unshackling of the ancient universities from the domination of the Church of England. The growth of popular education, most notably with the 1870 Forster Education Act, witnessed a clear secularization. Then again, Catholic Emancipation not only spelt religious freedom, it also effectively shifted influence once again away from the established Church. The advent of the theory of evolution, which was later given more credence with Mendel's work on genetics, further undermined naïve religious interpretations of the human world. Although Samuel Wilberforce's encounter with Thomas Huxley was not as melodramatic nor as crude as journalistic accounts have suggested, nonetheless the debate itself marks a passing of the high-water mark of the theological interpretation of human experience and society, which had dominated the scene from the early middle ages onward. Hints of this are also there from the point of view of theologians, in Benjamin Jowett's reflections in *Essays and Reviews*, which was published in 1860. Jowett notes towards the end of his reflections:

If anyone who is about to become a clergyman feels or thinks that he feels that some of the preceding statements cast a shade of trouble or suspicion on his future walk of life, who, either from the influence of a stronger mind than his own, or from some natural tendency in himself, has been led to examine those great questions which lie on the threshold of the higher study of theology, and experiences a sort of shrinking or dizziness at the prospect which is opening upon him; let him lay to heart the following consider-ations ... No man should busy himself with them who has not the cleanness of mind enough to see things as they are, and a faith strong enough to rest in that degree of knowledge which God has really given; or who is unable to separate the truth from his own religious wants and experiences.[8]

The critical edge which one can feel here is part of what made Jowett's book of essays so controversial at the time of its publication. It represents a shift in perception that is well documented in the imaginative literature of the period. George Eliot's Mr Casaubon, in *Middlemarch*, classically exemplifies the futile search for religious certainty and the final eclipse of that view which still saw theology as the 'queen of the sciences'. Eliot had herself been the translator of David Friedrich Strauss's famous sceptical *Life of Jesus*. Alongside this, she was the translator of Ludwig Feuerbach's *Essence of Christianity*. Feuerbach was to have a profound influence on Karl Marx, whose writings were also to offer a new interpretation of society which was largely antipathetic to Christian belief. Yet another famous barometer of this shift from belief within imaginative literature was Matthew Arnold's celebrated poem, *Dover Beach*, with its well known lines:

> The Sea of Faith
> Was once, too, at the full, and round earth's shore,
> Lay like the folds of a bright girdle furled.
> But now I only hear
> Its melancholy, long, withdrawing roar.

Although it would be facile to suggest that agnosticism and unbelief were rife, nevertheless, these trends undermined the previous tendency of theology to offer the most profound and convincing interpretation of contemporary events and their implications for the future. So to whom, then, had the baton been passed? Or, more subtly, which other interpreter began to challenge the theologians for this noble crown?

Perhaps the first and most obvious challenge came from the historian who began to move into his own with the flowering of Enlightenment thought in the eighteenth century. It was the ability to refer to source documents and to produce elements of critical historical study that gave to the Enlightenment much of its corrosive power. One could now begin to appreciate how things had come to be; one could leap onto the stage and look behind the scenes. Edward Gibbon's *Decline and Fall of the Roman Empire*, with its special implications for Christianity, is perhaps the perfect example of this. But the critical historical method had direct implications for Christianity itself. These same methods could now be applied to the biblical documents. In Germany, Samuel Reimarus' writings, from which G. E. Lessing published the notorious *Wolfenbüttel Fragments*, challenged the historicity of the gospels.

The point, however, is broader than issues of faith and unbelief. It is that history began to acquire for itself a 'scientific reputation' that gave it a claim to interpret human experience as it had not been able to do before. Indeed, theologians themselves were caught up into this very process. Even Edward Bouverie Pusey, who was later seen as the very essence of religious conservatism, was an English pioneer of the critical historical method in biblical study. John Henry Newman, too, saw the importance of historical study. His *Essay on the Development of Christian Doctrine* is effectively an application of the critical historical method, within the history of ideas, to the development of Christian doctrine. In his later work on the development of the intellectual tradition, *The Idea of a University*, Newman found this historical method requiring him now to defend theology as one of the sciences. He singles out Gibbon as the villain of the piece:

> Gibbon paints with pleasure what, conformably with the sentiments of a godless intellectualism, was an historical fulfilment of his own idea of moral perfection.[9]

The measure of Newman's defensiveness against the incursions of historical interpretation can be seen earlier on in the same book:

> ... I have urged that, supposing Theology be not taught, its province will not simply be neglected, but will actually be usurped by other sciences, which will teach, without warrant, conclusions of their own in a subject-matter which needs its own proper principles for its due formation and disposition.[10]

There is also a sense in which not only the intellectual discourse of history, but also significant breaks in continuity with the 'old world', left their mark upon history's ability to act as an interpreter. The most dramatic of these events was, of course, the French Revolution. The violence of the revolution, its shattering of the *ancien régime* and its deliberate shunning of the old objective moral order suggested the heralding of a new age. This terrifying shift could not be explained without reference to history and the use of the historical method as an interpreter. This interpretation, as with the older theological method, would have its implications for the present and the future. The French Revolution acted as a stimulus for a form of secular apocalyptic eschatology.

The influences of critical historical study cannot be underestimated. It has been seen by many as a new science and there is no doubting the potential relativizing effects of historical perspectives. But such methods have also brought with them a great sense of liberation. No longer can individuals or events from the past be used uncritically to legitimate injustices and inequalities in the present. Historical interpretation has contributed both a complete set of tools and a methodology, as human beings reflect upon their own experience and the future of civilization. In effect, some of the comment and analysis of current affairs is itself historical interpretation in the making. But is history a science or have historical analysis and interpretation now been eclipsed by the triumphs of science?

As we have already seen, the rise of modern science from Renaissance onward was part of that general movement that began to clip the wings of the prevailing theological interpretation within western culture. It was not until the nineteenth century, however, that the 'scientific bandwagon' would triumph with a great succession of discoveries and leaps in human understanding. Dalton's atomic theory of matter, early in the century, was followed by James Clark Maxwell's electromagnetic theory of radiation and then a little later by Darwin's theory of evolution. Much of this ability to produce new wide-ranging theories about the nature of matter and its effects upon our understanding of both the natural and human world was rooted in the growth of a new 'scientific method'. The Greek deductive approach to science which had held sway for two millennia gave way to the inductive method. Although in a crude form this inductive method has now been superseded, the process of inference from careful observation and experimentation remains central to the work of the scientific community.

Equally significant has been the use of these insights more generally. First of all, wide-ranging theories of matter place our human experience in context. The work of Max Planck and Albert Einstein in Quantum Theory and Relativity Theory was swiftly followed by the work of Werner Heisenberg on Uncertainty. The feeling of 'progress' that issued from nineteenth-century science offered, through these wide-ranging theories, another set of tools for interpreting our world and our experience. The optimism that could thus be generated was pinpointed fairly early on with the popular works of Herbert Spencer. Spencer was an exponent of the theory that 'progress is the supreme law of the universe'. Science, for Spencer, had transformed human capability and was the ground for this universal optimism. Science offered, through experiment and observation, a pre-dictability in our understanding of the universe pre-viously unavailable.

In the early part of the twentieth century, the tragic and meaningless suffering of the Great War put an end to such theories of progress. The underlying confidence in science, however, did not disappear. At a popular level, science continues to underpin the beliefs of many, that we can predict and to a large degree control the environment in which we live. The later development of the human sciences of psychology, sociology and economics added to this confidence, even though as disciplines there has never arisen quite such a feeling of 'objectiveness' as that spawned by the natural sciences in the nineteenth century. Even so, the extraordinary popularity of books like Stephen Hawking's *A Brief History of Time* suggests that scientific interpretation of our world remains a most potent force. It stands along-side the historical method in offering us another set of tools and a distinctive methodology. But has it not itself again been eclipsed? What has led to the discrediting of theories of progress and to the swift movement from one set of interpretations to another? Is it not the appear-ance of a new class of 'interpreters supreme' born of a world of instant communication and information tech-nology?

These brief reflections began with a quotation from John Simpson's fascinating account of his time as a television correspondent, who had found himself again and again on the front line both during the so-called 'velvet revolutions' in Eastern Europe in 1989, and in more violent encounters, including Tiananmen Square in Beijing. Simpson was able to relay to people across the world these events, even as they were unfolding. During the past forty years there has been a revolution in the capacity of the media, in communications generally, and in information processing. In the mid-1950s, soon after her coronation, Her Majesty The Queen embarked upon a series of demanding tours of 'her dominions'. Even then, the film and newsreel material revealed worlds unknown to western civilization. But it is doubtful now whether any such unknown worlds still exist. The information and media revolution has collapsed the size of our world.

This alone has meant that the instant interpretation of newspapers, radio and television has had a powerful impact upon our corporate self-consciousness. It is easy for our minds to be made up for us, even before we have heard the news. The media have enormous power to interpret our world for us. Three examples – one positive, one more neutral and one negative – may make the point. First a positive example. It was the televising of vivid and tragic pictures from Ethiopia in 1989 and 1990 that finally galvanized the western nations into responding to the terrible famine there. Public opinion was transformed by the transmission of those devastating images and governments were forced to act.

The second, more neutral, example takes us to Iceland. Only 250,000 people live in Iceland, and probably as many Icelanders live elsewhere in the world. The small number of people constituting a nation, combined with media bombardment in English from the western side of the Atlantic, is posing a threat to the future of Icelandic as a language. Interpretation and communication are increasingly happening in English. It is the media interpreters who have set the pace and who may decide the fate of the Icelandic tongue. A similar point could be made about Gaelic in the Scottish Western Isles.

The final, and most negative, example relates to the manner in which the British press have handled the Royal Family and particularly the former Princess of Wales. Even a republican would have to admit that not only privacy but also the public's ability to discern a fair interpretation of people and events has been severely distorted by much of the media presentation. During the week following the death of Princess Diana it was difficult to discern precisely when public opinion was being decided in advance by the press. The reaction from the public to her death and the events preceding and following it have indicated that the media will not be allowed uncritically to be the sole interpreters of human experience and contemporary society.

Is our desire to 'see ourselves' through different interpreters primarily a form of 'corporate narcissism' or is it instead a real seeking after insight and corporate self-knowledge – or is it a little of each? Looking back over these reflections, it does feel more like a question of self-knowledge, and one might loosely argue that in different periods of history, different groups hold sway as the key interpreters of our world. Until the dawn of the Enlightenment, the power of the Church and the influence of theologians was indeed crucial and perhaps decisive. Early on in the Enlightenment, historical interpretation began to become increasingly significant. In the late nineteenth and early twentieth century it fell to scientists to offer a similar critique. Now the media rule OK. But such an analysis is too crude by far. The situation is now far more complex. The growth of critical attitudes to the analysis of human experience has sharpened humanity's self-transcendence. Different disciplines and groups vie with each other in helping us to 'see ourselves'. Which groups can offer the most convincing argument that they have the decisive say in the interpretation of contemporary society? The following four contributions may help you to decide the answer to that question. Or, conversely, you may feel that yet another group is the key to this fascinating question. Or is the jury still out?

Stephen Platten

Notes

1. John Simpson, *The Darkness Crumbles: Despatches from the Barricades Revised and Updated*, Hutchinson, London, 1992, p. 356
2. Mark 13:24–27 (R.S.V.)
3. I Corinthians 10:11
4. cf particularly the excellent account in Robin Lane Fox, *Pagans and Christians*, Viking, Harmondsworth, 1986
5. Bede, *Ecclesiastical History of the English People*, translated by Leo Sherley-Price, Penguin, Harmondsworth, revised edition 1990

6. op. cit. p. 147
7. Alasdair MacIntyre, *After Virtue*, Duckworth, London, 1981
8. *Essays and Reviews*, John W. Parker, London 1860. 'Essay on the Interpretation of Scripture', by Benjamin Jowett, page 430
9. John Henry Newman, *The Idea of a University*, Holt, Rinehart and Winston, New York, 1960, p. 149
10. op. cit. p. 74

Seeing Ourselves:
The Journalist's Perspective

LIBBY PURVES

Many people tend to think of the media as interpreting our age for us. We live in an extraordinary age of instant social history. I suppose once upon a time there was a golden age when commentators waited twenty years, or even fifty, and looked at all the indicators, at what happened and what was said, before they announced that on such and such a date 'a new era' began. Today, new eras happen overnight. The new Britain is trumpeted once a decade at least. You may remember the new Sixties' Britain, when we were told that we were suddenly a swinging nation of hot liberated chicks and no more class distinctions. There is a whole generation now adult who grew up in the suburbs and provincial towns in those sixties and are still indignant that they seem to have missed it all. They got married much as their parents did, joined the Rotary Club, and never even got to see Mary Quant. They tell their children, 'Well, I had one of those Vidal Sassoon haircuts with a V at the back of my neck, but it was done in Ipswich and it never quite worked really.'

More recently, we had the new Thatcher Britain – peopled with all these semi-mythical beasts like yuppies,

Essex men and Sloane Rangers, and fashion victims. The 'me generation' was announced in bold, showy head-lines, and also the style generation. We were told that universal tolerance was trendy but that mutual aid and support, family life and old-fashioned things like that were boring, yawnie concepts. Not condemning others became groovily politically correct, while actually help-ing others practically, or putting their interests before yours, was boring, po-faced, timid do-goodery to be mocked.

Yet this period was also a time when charities flourished in Britain as never before, and when, despite all that the media told us about the grinding supremacy of political correctness, racial violence also flourished. So, those weren't entirely true interpretations either. And now, weary of all this, we are apparently, so we have been hearing since the Election and the death of Diana Princess of Wales, living suddenly in a new carey, sharey, Blairy Britain, whose patron saint is Diana in her most compassionate and mature phase. We are all 'touchy and feely' now – we're returning to the family, to concepts of beauty, altruism and kindness, and taller, thinner typefaces in the new *Independent* headlines (it all goes together, in the fevered mind of the journalist). We are rediscovering community – the General Election proves that surely! The crowds in Kensington Gardens prove that. Compassion, as the fashion editors would put it, is the new navy blue.

Unfortunately, as usual, the instant social history is a little bit too good for the facts. There were very few journalists, indeed, who dared in the general hysteria to point out the fact that all those people walking towards Kensington Palace, with flowers in homage to the new saint of Centrepoint and compassion, were completely ignoring the homeless people in the cardboard boxes underneath their very feet.

But this instant history, this self-conscious running commentary on how we are as a nation, is something which is fed to us constantly from a thousand tributaries. It comes from newspapers, from magazines and the supplements they spawn, from the journalistic quick-fix books they serialize – because I think we must include in the concept of journalism a great many things which are classified as books because they happen to have covers. There was a time when writing a book was considered a rather serious, scholarly, 'go away and research it for years' thing to do. These days, if you have even one mildly good idea, somebody will spring on you to do a book: *The Five-Minute Father*, *The Five-Minute Manager*, *Why Women are Unhappy*, *Why Men are Unhappy* or *Britain on the Couch* etc. I cannot count the number of times I have written an 800-word column in something like the *Sunday Express* (years ago I used to work for them) and had three letters from publishers saying 'There's a book in this concept.' And I would say, 'I'm sorry, there were 800 words in that concept – it was quite fun but even keeping it going that long was a bit of a strain!' Publishers can become quite aggressive about this. So remember, when I refer to journalism in this interpretative sense I am talking about a great many of these instant books.

A running commentary on what we are and what we

are becoming is also fed to us by politicians and political people. Some of them are genuinely high-minded reformers and mean every word of it. Some of them are cynical opportunists and don't mean any of it. Telling them apart is the tricky bit. But a great deal of this interpretation is complete bunk. Nations do not change on a whim. The slow evolution of the way we think and behave is a gradual process – one step forward, two steps back, one sideways, two forward. That kind of change in how we are, and how we think is driven by very complex forces: economics, changes in medicine, advancing technology and pharmaceuticals.

Women's changing social position has been influenced probably just as much by an efficient generation of contraceptives as it ever was by suffragettes. Developments in transport and education and patterns of industrialization have altered our concept of the extended family every bit as much as Freud did, or Bertrand Russell. A classic example: the middle classes didn't suddenly give up living in the same neighbourhood as their extended families because of an ideological upsurge of intellectual individualism or conscious objection to old tribal values. People got scattered because of jobs, and because of kids going away to university and getting used to the idea of living at the other end of the country. They got scattered by motorways and new towns and house prices and the patterns of the building of big factories. Companies these days think that it is their right to relocate people. They don't say that they make them sell their house, uproot themselves and go and live at the other end of the country, with or without their reluctant spouse. No, it's just called relocating: it's another management tool, like downsizing.

So, you can't say that it was changes in attitude, changes in belief, which caused particular huge tranches of social change to happen – it was largely practical things. The working class communities didn't split up of their own accord either. In some areas at least they were shifted by main force, by governments that could not see the point of the unseen values of community. And even when a trend, a change of attitude, a change in us, is real, it proceeds at different speeds and down different paths in different parts of the country.

Now, I live in Suffolk, and I do live properly in Suffolk. I have no London flat or London home, as people tend sometimes to assume when I write for a newspaper based in London. I have a gismo on my computer which squirts stuff through to London and I go up once a week to the BBC. I sit in Suffolk and I often gasp at the way that North London journalists constantly assure me in print that everyone is doing some particular thing. They will suddenly announce the death of the dinner party, or tell you that all young professionals use cannabis routinely, or that the New Man is completely extinct and men have given up that business of doing things with their young children.

More seriously, because it then affects behaviour through what they write and say, they will say things like 'There is nowhere that women are safe on the streets at night.' I remember a particular instance when *The Times* carried an utterly hysterical piece by a London woman journalist after the murder on the M3. It said that no female could any longer go out alone after dusk. As it happened, we were sailing round Britain at the time with our young children, and I read this in Weymouth in a launderette at ten o'clock in the evening. When I had finished my washing some very kind skinheads carried it back down to the quay for me and we nattered a bit about the weather. I felt at that moment as if I lived on a different planet, not just planet Dorset as against planet London, but reality as against some kind of fictional newspaper-land, a fictional composite newspaper-land, from where the views were coming with incredible eloquence. The same feeling assails me when there is a child murder and the whole nation gasps – as well we should. But instead of praying for that child and its family, thinking of them and hoping that particular crime is soon solved, the pundits tell us that none of our children are safe anywhere because the streets are crawling with paedophiles. In fact, the murder of a child by a stranger is the very, very rarest crime there is. Child murder is, alas, usually a family crime, and the most common crime with a child victim is bicycle theft. This is not a fact that often appears in newspapers.

But then random crime of every kind is vastly over-feared by the British today. Nobody would deny that there are black spots and grim estates. But whenever you do a survey on fear of crime, it suggests that for every person who dreads the streets and open spaces because they have experienced crime or their friends have, there are dozens of others who have never met crime personally, but have met it constantly, vicariously, through the media and worry 'because of the terrible things you read in the papers and see on the telly'.

These are just examples pulled out of the air to show how distorting a mirror journalism can become; and I should say here that I do particularly mean national journalism. Local journalism is different, though God knows it has its faults (the strange bragging way in which local newspapers always speak – 'Multiple Murder in Local Town', 'Local Man Banged up for Twenty Years', and so on). I think, on the whole, that local journalism and local media are exempt from a lot of distortion simply because it is quite possible for their listeners, viewers and readers to come round and grumble personally, and they do. I always remember on Radio Oxford the salutary experience of reading (and I hadn't written this – I was just reading it) a news bulletin about a strike at British Leyland and staggering out of the studio at ten past seven in the morning – we never locked the doors in those days – to find three large Leyland blokes saying, 'We've just come to tell you that that six o'clock bulletin was all wrong.' That is how it really is, and I thought yes, this is my kind of journalism. I like it when people fight back.

So the distortions I am talking about are primarily national press and media distortions, and though the mirror is distorting it is very persuasive; because frankly in Britain today journalism is extremely skilled. There are brilliant descriptive writers practising the trade and this applies all the way through every grade of newspaper. And there are also brilliant polemicists. I have quite often got carried away reading some highly charged emotional piece, only to put it down and reflect five minutes later that it is entirely wrong – that its case is extrapolated from one example, that example sometimes semi-fictionalized with heart-jerking descriptions, and that it has thus built a case which does not accord with the complex daily reality of the issue on the ground. Sometimes partisan journalism – and I am sure I have done this too – invents its own enemies so that it can knock them down more resoundingly.

There was a wonderful classic of this recently. Tony Blair, the Prime Minister, has said that he wants every single mother at least to attend a job centre and look at possibilities once her children are of school age, over five. Now there was a piece strongly attacking this initiative. It gave a heart-wringing example of a young woman known to the author who had just had a baby and planned to go back after her maternity leave when it was six months old. 'Now,' said the writer, 'this poor young woman, almost a child herself, couldn't bear to leave her baby. Is it fair to force her to?' and he mentioned that there is a project in Wisconsin in the United States where young mothers are made to go and look for jobs. What was that? Wisconsin? Nobody in this country had said that young mothers of tiny children, pre-school children, should be driven into factories and made to dump their children in state crèches.[1] And yet the example round which the piece was built was quite woefully misleading. In the real world, there is all the difference between separating mothers and tiny children on pain of starving them to death, and asking mothers of thumping great schoolchildren of ten or thirteen to do some part-time work during school hours instead of pottering around at home feeling bored and broken, marginalized and watching day-time television. Yet the piece was well sewn together. If the author's aim was to portray the current Government as heartless, Soviet-style, social engineers, he did well. But all he was doing was shadow-boxing.

But, I say it again, our standards of journalism are high. Even ethically, they are quite high. (I have to admit that I don't know how some editors can bear to wake up in the same bed as themselves in the morning.) Let us say, ethically, quite high, with lapses. Technically, which is almost more important when it comes to the effectiveness of the mirror, the standards are very high. We in the media have our problems of taste, we have our problems of intrusion, we have problems of over-enthusiasm for getting stories at the expense of respectable human behaviour. But as a tribe we, the journalists, have kept the nation informed about many things the nation should be informed about, whether it's Dunblane, or the astonishing revelations in the Scott Enquiry about how we are governed and with how much contempt, or whether it's BSE, which journalists like the BBC's Derek Cooper pinpointed four years before the government acknowledged it. Journalists have shown us the state of some of our worst inner cities, the inspiring behaviour of the fathers who lost their children to IRA bombers and still attempted to talk to the IRA of peace, and Bosnia, Somalia and the persecution of the Iraqi Kurds, and the elections in South Africa. Journalists made sure you knew about it. You felt for it, you shared in it, perhaps you gave money to alleviate the suffering of it because of journalists. We cannot do without their mirror, in spite of its flaws.

So, if you have a flawed mirror it is worth knowing what the sources of distortion in it are, and allowing for them. I thought tonight that I would consider what I think are prime sources of distortion; and, thinking about them, I found myself to my surprise rather discounting the obvious ones. Like the legend that there are evil proprietors with secret agendas and systematic bias and all the rest of it. I found myself, rather, dividing the sources into four, some of which may seem small but which, nonetheless, can create wide anomalies. The first of them is quite simple – it's *speed*. I shouldn't have to say this to an audience that knows what's what, but in fact I even have to say it to myself – to remind myself of how much can be excused by the problem of speed, by how fast it all happens. In the early days of broadcast news, the head of news said to his troops, 'I don't care about being first – I do care about being right.' But at that time there was no opposition – there was no rivalry. Now, the urge to be first is intensely strong for broadcasters, and so is the need to fill allocated space. If there is a big story your instinct is to give it big time. But you may know very little about the big story, and still be compelled to recognize its importance. You can't say in one line: 'The Archbishop of Canterbury is said to have eloped with a chorus girl – more news as it comes in' and then go on to the Liberal Party Conference, can you? You have to make the story important, so you have to say, 'The Archbishop of Canterbury is said to have eloped with a chorus girl – more news as it comes

in' and then, 'And now over to our Archbishop corre-
spondent/over to our church correspondent/over to our
chorus girl correspondent/our theatre correspondent,'
who then speaks and explains how long the show has
been running, and all the rest of it. However little you
know, you're still expected to fill the time, to speculate,
to talk to experts in allied areas, and sometimes the
result of this is a triumphantly rapid enlightenment. And
sometimes it is absolute tosh. I don't like to say this
because I have great loyalty to the BBC and revere it
in every way, but a great deal of what we were given
on Gulf FM, when it was suddenly decided that the
Gulf War would be covered by non-stop radio, was
complete tosh. You had generals predicting and specu-
lating, and every channel had its own general hired in
permanently, but all the things that actually happened
in the Gulf War – the firing of the oil fields for example
– were never predicted at all. Somebody once asked,
what four things had happened in the Gulf War, and
they listed them, led by the firing of the oil fields. None
of those four things had ever been predicted by any of
the pundits. With luck, the experts who are pulled in in
these circumstances, and pulled in at very short notice
(pulled in on the phone, or by a radio car parking outside
their house), have got the sense to say when they just
don't know the answer. Some are tempted, being
human, by excitement or vanity to speculate further
than is sensible. Sometimes they are tempted to speculate
further than is decent.

So, speed can distort in broadcasting. But then you
have the different pressure of speed on newspapers –

equally taxing and almost more productive of neurosis. Newspapers do not have the more natural pace of broadcasting, where the moment you know something you can put it on the air. The paper goes to bed at a set time. Every minute that it is late costs it thousands of pounds in an already cut-throat trade. Every story that is missed because you go to bed more or less on time is missed for twenty-four hours – during which the very professional, very highly motivated, very ambitious staff of those newspapers have to listen to the broadcasters giving new news. So, on a newspaper you have to get your facts straight, and marshalled, and their significance weighed, very, very fast indeed on some stories. And because you are skilled, because you are a very skilled, technically brilliant newspaper, whatever you print looks really good. It looks very convincing, it gets taken up by later editions of other newspapers and evening papers, and picked up by broadcasters. In this way distortion happens very easily.

This, of course, leads on to the second distortion – *reactive distortion*. I cannot recommend Paul Donovan's *The History of the Today Programme* too highly, for laughs! Here is something which is told by the MP Austin Mitchell, which explains exactly the kind of thing that can happen.

I wrote an article for the *New Statesman* about Labour's document *The Road to the Manifesto*. It tried to explain to party members who felt they weren't being consulted why things were as they were. It basically argued that we had to be beyond party members, we couldn't frighten people, we couldn't impose a radical manifesto because it could be used against us. I did quote in that article a party member who I didn't name but who'd asked me jokingly – what was the difference between our policy processes and those of Kim-il-Sung? It was just a remark made at a meeting.

Well, to cut a long story short, the magazine appeared on the Wednesday night, the *Today* programme rang up and invited him on a discussion, then cancelled him, and then suddenly, late at night, rang again because it turned out that the *Independent* newspaper had got hold of the *New Statesman* article and put it on the front page, interpreting it as an attack on Tony Blair in the comparison of him with the Korean dictator Kim-il-Sung, which it wasn't. But the *Today* programme was reacting to this.

They were reacting not to my views but to the distortion of those views in the *Independent*. I did a phone interview with John Humphries the following morning. It seemed to baffle him that I was in fact very supportive of the leadership. When asked what I wanted to get out of it, I said a job. I went back to bed, having put the phone down, and it suddenly became red hot because all the other media were listening to *Today* and they'd either heard this or seen the front page of the *Independent*. I think probably they were responding to *Today*. So Sky News, BBC,

ITN, Radio Humberside all rang wanting to do interviews.

When I got up and prepared to sally out, Michael Heseltine had been brought onto the *Today* programme and chortled away. 'Kim-il-Sung, Kim-il-Sung,' he kept saying, 'that's a bit rich. No-one's ever called John Major Kim-il-Sung.' Robin Cook was asked his opinion and he said, 'Well, Austin Mitchell's a serial maverick.' John Major even referred to it in his conference speech about how some people called Tony Blair Kim-il-Sung. Ever since then people have been writing me letters and abusing me and saying, 'Why did you call Tony Blair Kim-il-Sung? I left the party in '82 to get away from wreckers like you.' I've been asked by the party's press officer not to give any more interviews on the grounds that it would give the story legs and keep it alive. I wasn't therefore able to point out that I've never called Tony Blair Kim-il-Sung. I haven't even mentioned them in the same sentence, or the same paragraph. I think this demonstrates the infuriating power of the *Today* programme. My career ruined – my future in the Labour Party wrecked – and all because of the *Today* programme!

It's a sad little story that. It's a small and unimportant political example, but it happens with stories of all kinds. Somebody says something or there is a report which includes something a little bit provocative, and the journalist in a hurry rings up someone who is likely to disagree or disapprove, and this person gives a comment, not on the basis of the actual report or article or the words spoken, because they haven't seen the whole of it. Maybe they don't have a fax. Canny people say, 'Fax me the whole text.' But then the journalist just goes and rings someone else – it's quicker. And so their disapproval is blazoned and becomes the story. Suppose, say, the Dean of Norwich says in a local radio interview that he hasn't been getting much work done lately at home because of the noise of repair work on the west end of the chancel. But it's more than worth it to think the roof will be restored at last! So somebody from a news agency picks that up and the reporter has an idea and rings up a couple of local residents to say, 'Do you think the noise is worth it?' (Of course this wouldn't be Norwich because Norwich is always in such perfect repair anyway!) But he captures these residents at a bad moment and they say, 'Certainly not, it's been driving us crazy!' So the reporter rings up the Bishop to see if he is happy about the repair work. The Bishop, unaware that there's a row, says, 'Yes, it's splendid, at last we'll be able to see the gargoyles properly again.' Then the reporter says, 'It's a bit tough on the poor Dean. His house is very close to the noise.' The Bishop and Dean are friends, so the Bishop laughs and says, 'Oh, let him suffer – do him good!' So now the reporter has got a lovely story – 'Let Them Suffer, Says Bishop' – 'Uncaring Churchman Shrugs Off Torment of Old Lady's Sleepless Nights and Says He'd Rather Have Gargoyles.' So there you go, a storm in a teacup. If the hapless prelate is quick to apologize next day, frog-marched into it by a press officer, then you get 'Banging Bishop Forced into U-turn'.

And that's a distortion. It happens every day. It happens to politicians, it happens to people in public life, and that is why the canny ones employ public relations men and women, and spin doctors of Mandelsonian skill.

And this leads to the third distortion. We've had speed, and we've had reactive distortion and now we have *spin and PR*. Now don't underestimate this. Journalists at the very top of the trade pretend to be canny and clever and pretty contemptuous of spin-doctors – 'we can see through them'. But there's a great deal of money and a great deal of brains — because you can buy brains with money – that go into the trade of manipulating news and news features. In a busy newsroom of any kind – and remember that a lot of newsrooms are understaffed because either they are commercial organizations, or they are organizations which are being made to ape commercial organizations in their working practices – in a busy, possibly slightly understaffed newsroom, a well-written press release is a godsend. It's easy to re-write, it's got some ready-made wit and angle in it and you can ring up somebody and they'll give you even more wit and angle. So it's a godsend – you get your story in. That's the most basic form of spin.

Two years ago I did a little book for children to try and alert seven-year-olds to the way the press works because I thought no-one had ever explained photo opportunities to seven-year-olds before, and I gave them a little exercise. Guess who might have fed these stories to a newspaper: 'Teachers Attack Government's Education Reforms' – 'Government Attacks Teachers' – 'New Electric Bicycle Invented by Norwich Firm' –

'Hollywood Star to Appear in New TV Series' – 'Young Disabled on the Movie Warpath: Why Can't We Take Wheelchairs into Cinema?' Now look at the newspaper, I said, and guess who might have fed those stories in. Look through a real newspaper and try and find three stories which would have come from the diary (I had explained the newsroom diary to them previously) and three which would have been fed to the newspaper by someone who wants publicity. And then I gave them a little exercise to do. 'Your school is going to do a ten-mile sponsored hop in fancy dress. Write a short press release to capture the attention of a busy editor and get some publicity in the paper. Perhaps it would help if you described one of the fancy dress costumes, or if you promised that some famous person would hop with you.' Does it matter if the famous person actually turns up? Does it hell! The children, even at seven years old, thought that this was very funny and sneaky, and a good game. They wrote some wonderful press releases for me when I went and did a session in a library with them.

I am happy to say that this kind of exercise, in sourcing stories and seeing who they're good for, actually comes into the history curriculum these days. Education is always attacking the history curriculum and saying it hasn't got enough heroes in it, but I've been very impressed by the history book my daughter, at nine, used to bring home from school, which had a story of Alfred and the cakes and a list of questions underneath saying, 'Who might have liked this story to get around? Where do you think it might have come from?' The new generation needs such lessons.

Turning the screw a bit further than the mere press release, there's more elaborate PR. There are parties and tempting introductions to stars, and the lure of glamour. If you write a press release saying that Arnie Schwarzenegger and Sylvester Stalone are coming over to open Planet Hollywood, their new burger restaurant in central London, that is cheaper than taking out a full-page advertisement for your burger restaurant in central London, and far more effective. And there are glamorous launches and gimmicky launches, things with stories attached; the kind of thing which, although the paper and the media know perfectly well is a stunt, it is a good stunt and will cheer the bulletin up that day. So they will use it, often fairly uncritically because the same public relations firm will be inviting them to another good stunt the following week. And then there's the opposite of the big launch – there are the private lunches, where the great and the good (sometimes even the royal) take individual journalists to lunch and draw them into feeling like an insider. They feed little titbits about the corridors of power – on a lobby basis, of course, not formally. In return for this they hope that you will think them nice people and slant any story involving them in a way that reflects well on them, or at least reflects well on their intentions and character.

Two things make this very effective. One is old-fashioned charm and the other is a sort of insidious insiderishness. My favourite description of how it works is not in a journalistic context at all, but the context of a young academic being corrupted by an evil research institute. It is in C. S. Lewis's curious novel *That Hideous Strength*. This is the moment:

> This was the first thing Mark had been asked to do which he himself before he did it, clearly knew to be criminal. But the moment of his consent almost escaped his notice – certainly there was no struggle, no sense of turning a corner. There may have been a time in the world's history when such moments fully revealed their gravity, with witches prophesying on a blasted heath or visible rubicons to be crossed. But to him it all slipped past in a chatter of laughter – of that intimate laughter between fellow-professionals, which of all earthly powers is strongest to make men to do very bad things before they are yet individually very bad men.

The inside track, the inner ring, the sense of being one of those in the know, can sometimes stop journalists from passing on all that they know. Or from putting a slant on it which their basic humanity should show them is in fact the right slant.

So, there is speed, there is spin, there is the reactive thing, and then there is *geography*. National journalism is overwhelmingly metropolitan. Newspapers may be Manchester-based or Glasgow-based but are mainly London-based. And I think this creates distortion, too. I think the classic example is over country matters. Country matters have tended to be reflected largely in the national press by rather blimpish, tweedy characters, particularly those with the kind of penchant for field sports that is instinctive and racial, rather than thought through. I think this is improving – the countryside as an issue is at last being properly represented to town readers by several papers – but when it comes to the quieter issues, to matters like housing and poverty, there is a difficulty of emphasis. The country speakers and arguers tend to be more uncomplaining, less emphatic and far less strident than the voice of the city. Their interests easily get drowned, especially in very tall windowless towers in the middle of London. There are countless glossy magazines giving the impression that the countryside is a permanent glorious idyll and that anybody who lives there is either damn lucky or rich enough to buy designer garden trugs, and therefore has nothing to complain about. *The Archers* doesn't help either, but at least it doesn't claim to be journalism. I think here local media, local radio, local broadcasting and regional broadcasting, too, have helped a great deal, but I also think that central broadcasters – all right, the BBC – tend not to listen properly to the voices coming up from the regions. There is a slight spat going on at the moment because of some ill-judged remarks made by the Head of BBC News, Tony Hall, to the effect that during the Diana week they were all 'astonished' and learnt a great deal from the amazing articulateness and honesty and the quality of the voices of ordinary people. He said that the BBC simply had to learn that ordinary people did have interesting, valid and moving things to say. Quite correctly, some local broadcasters have written in to say, 'We knew this – we have been talking to them for years. Why haven't you? Why did you think it more appropriate to talk to Andrew Neil about how the nation felt?' Local media were very irritated indeed by Mr Hall's wondering tone.

Finally, there is something else. There is the *culture* of journalism – the culture of comment without responsibility and polemic without practical politics, and journalism's awkwardly high status. It seems to me one of the most extraordinary things that has happened over the last two decades is that young people, who would once have wanted to go into law, or business, or banking, or teaching, have aspired above everything else to journalism. Half the 'A' level students in this country at some stage considered doing media studies. Virtually millions, when asked what they want to do as a career in the sixth form, will say journalism. Now this is a curious culture, if you think about it. There is no job security in journalism (or hardly any, unless you become a sort of powerful, controversial editor of a down-market Sunday tabloid and you keep on getting sacked and getting big redundancy money, and then being the editor of another one and getting sacked again). There is no power in journalism – there's no control over events. There is just the power of commenting and reporting. Even reporting gets down-graded with the rise of the columnists and analysts. I have never been more shocked in my life than when I went to the Cambridge Union to meet the *crème de la crème* of youth, and I said 'What's the buzz? What's happening? What does everybody want to do? How do you want to save the world?' because I was remembering myself as a student in the sixties, all bright eyed and bushy tailed and wanting to be something real. And the then President of the Cambridge Union (I can't remember the year, so his identity is safe and his blushes spared) said that he really wanted to be a constitutional expert. And I said, 'What, some kind of academic?' And he said, 'No, I'd like to be somebody who gets asked to be on television to comment on the royal family and stuff.' I thought he was joking and looked closely at him, and he wasn't joking at all. He wanted to be a telly don, so even though he was going to try and go on to be a university don, he wanted to be the kind of university don that was always on television. That was the main point – he wanted to be a commentating journalist. His final ambition was one day to be on *The Moral Maze*.

Even though I am a columnist – and I say to you that I did not ask to be one, I never asked, I thought I was a feature-writing reporter – I find the culture unsettling. As Matthew Parris once said, there is a prevailing culture in the country, of people who can't mend a wheelbarrow, feeling themselves able to have views on how to run the country. There are too many journalists who have never managed a whelk stall for an afternoon, yet who tell the CBI how to manage its affairs. There are plenty who have never sorted out a fight even between two children over the age of three, who think they can lecture the Government about what to do about Bosnia. There are journalists who have chaotic and disgraceful private lives, who think they can lecture film stars or the Windsors on their private lives. This I think is a problem, and the thing that makes it even more of a distortion is the cult of the personality journalist. In the old days most people didn't ever have a by-line. News editors would say to young reporters, 'We don't want to know how you felt about being at the fire. Forget that, lad, just tell us what the fire burnt.' But now, the more of yourself you put in it, the more outrageous the things you say, then the better known you get. That has to lead to distortion – showing off always does.

I think that all these main distortions need comment, and need thought, and need challenging quite loudly – and if possible humorously – by readers and consumers of the media. That's your job. Do it!

Note

1. This example was given in the months before it became clear that Labour did indeed intend to cut support to mothers of pre-school children. At the time of the lecture such an expansion of the policy seemed incredible.

Seeing Ourselves:
The Historian's Perspective

ROBERT BLAKE

It is an honour and a pleasure to give a lecture in this series in memory of Launcelot Fleming. I knew him, liked him and greatly respected him. He was a man of courage, clear mind and deep social sympathy. Others will have paid a fuller tribute to his career, so I will simply leave it at that rather than repeat what they have said.

History and historians are, and always have been, highly controversial subjects and sometimes receive more brickbats than praise. Gibbon famously described history as little more than 'the register of the crimes, follies and misfortunes of mankind'. On historians, A. J. P. Taylor observed, 'History does not repeat itself, but historians repeat each other.' Neither of these dicta is entirely true. Even Gibbon recognized, in his account of the Age of the Antonines, that the Roman Empire's history was not entirely criminal, foolish and unlucky. And Taylor certainly claimed that in some of his works, especially his very controversial account of the origins of the Second World War, he was breaking new ground and not ploughing familiar fields. Whether the resultant crop was good or bad is another matter.

I do not think that most historians set about their task with a view to interpreting contemporary society. They are of course a part of, and influenced by, the society in which they live. This is why the history of historiography is such a fascinating subject. Gibbon was an eighteenth-century sceptic, Macaulay an early-nineteenth-century Whig. Their interpretation of the past was to some degree affected by their own present, but they were not trying to explain the nature of the social, economic and spiritual world around them. They were trying to re-create, conjure up, depict and bring to life the vanished world which they studied. If it had implications for their contemporary world that was a by-product, perhaps a bonus, but not the main purpose, which has always been to describe and explain the past, not to analyse the present, let alone predict the future. And this is a fascinating subject in its own right. Gibbon, in a footnote, sums up the feeling of a historian trying to re-create the past. He is referring to the preparations by the Byzantine general Belisarius for the invasion of Africa as described by a contemporary historian pointing out the importance of a then despised and underestimated force – the archers. 'How concise – how just – how beautiful is the whole picture! I see the attitude of the archer – I hear the twanging of the bow.'[1] It reminds me of one of the best of all TV films, Laurence Olivier's *Henry V*. Also, though arrows were not involved, of one of the best books on war – John Keegan's *The Face of Battle* – marvellous descriptions of the Battle of the Somme as well as Waterloo and others.

If, as I believe, historians are mainly concerned with telling the story of the past and making it come alive, this does not mean that their works have no bearing on the present and its problems. The three greatest of these for Britain are Northern Ireland, the Welfare State and Europe. I do not see how one can understand any of these without some knowledge of their past. To those who lack that knowledge what happens in Ireland with its repercussions in England must seem totally incomprehensible. It is easier to understand if one has read some account of the Irish 'plantations', of Cromwell at Drogheda, of the Battle of the Boyne, the Irish Rebellion, the career of O'Connell, the Famine, Parnell, the Easter Rising, the Treaty of 1922. It helps to explain those bowler hats and orange sashes worn by those who parade in seemingly pointless marches.

Of course, you do not need to have read all the gigantic literature on this depressing hag-ridden subject, but you need to have some degree of non-partisan knowledge. History as taught in Eire, and Catholic Schools in Ulster, is unrecognizable in Protestant schools. And the way history is taught to the young on both sides of the great divide merely serves to reinforce tribal and atavistic attitudes. A wealthy friend of mine has been prepared to finance the publication of a series of non-partisan and impartial school history text books in the hope of breaking through the cultural barrier. I hope he succeeds. He has recruited some very good people as writers and editors, but I do not as yet know just how far he has got.

*　　　*　　　*

And who can understand the problems of the Welfare State without at least some knowledge of its history from Lloyd George, through Beveridge, to the present day? The same applies to 'Europe'. It is very difficult to find a clear and concise account of how the European idea has developed since the Treaty of Rome. This is partly because the subject is gigantically complicated and befogged by an obscure jargon of what is called 'Euro-speak' in which everything seems to mean the opposite of what it says. A lucid history of all this would be invaluable, but as difficult to achieve as one of Ulster. My basic point is that a proper and impartial history of Ulster, the Welfare State and 'Europe' – the three great problems of our time – needs the elucidation of historians.

Historians cannot solve these problems. But they can perhaps draw attention to the difficulties of solving them, even the impossibility of doing so in some cases. The Prime Minister, Lord Salisbury, long before he came into power, wrote:

The optimist view of politics assumes that there must be some remedy for every political ill, and rather than not find it, will make two hardships to cure one ... But is not the other view barely possible? Is it not just conceivable that there is no remedy that we can apply to the Irish hatred of ourselves, that other loves or hates may possibly some day elbow it out of the Irish peasants' mind, that nothing we can do by any contrivance will hasten the advent of that period?[2]

It is a depressing thought, but no-one who has studied history will fail to recognize that insoluble problems have existed and still do.

A similar problem very much in the news is Kashmir – in some ways India's and Pakistan's Ulster. An informed reading of the history of that unhappy province might have made those who advise the Queen more aware of the extreme sensitivities involved – particularly for a Labour government. It was Attlee's cabinet that agreed in 1947 to Mountbatten's allocation of a predominantly Muslim state to India. Indians are bitterly resentful of anything that looks like backtracking on this by a New Labour government that, they believe, is seeking to con-solidate support from the Pakistani vote in England – a vote more sympathetic to Labour than the Indian vote which tends towards Conservatism.

Another troubled spot of less direct relevance to Britain, but where a knowledge of history is important, is the lands known now as 'former Yugoslavia'. They are not entirely irrelevant. British soldiers are involved and some have been killed or wounded. But it is true that no British 'interest' in the old sense of national, commercial or strategic is involved. Yet who can say that this will remain the case? It is as well to know why and how the bitter hostility between Serbs, Croats, Albanians and Muslims came into being and what it was and is that makes co-existence seemingly impossible. It is an enormously complicated subject. There is an admirable history of Bosnia by Noel Malcolm which ought to be required reading for the Foreign Office and the Ministry of Defence. I doubt if it is.

Are there 'lessons' to be learnt from history? I think there are. But people do not always learn the right ones. Perhaps I can deviate into some personal reminiscences. In 1959, I was much involved with advising Anthony Eden on the writing of his memoirs. He was being paid £100,000 by *The Times* to serialize them – above all the volume (first to be published but last in chronological coverage) *Full Circle*, his version of his premiership and the Suez Crisis. This was a matter of intense controversy at the time and has been, with diminishing passion, ever since.

I supported Suez in 1956 and spoke to the local Oxford Conservative Association to that effect, making myself very unpopular in the Common Rooms of many colleges. I soon saw that, whatever the motives of Anglo-French action, it had been a total fiasco. Why did Eden do it? The decision was very much his personal one. Why not play the whole crisis long and slow? Nasser posed no immediate threat. The Egyptian pilots whom he substituted for Europeans were just as good at navigating the Canal as their displaced predecessors. It was not a difficult job anyway. And Nasser had no possible interest in blocking the traffic. Nor had he acted illegally, though some people argued otherwise.

But Eden came out in conversation – one never asked anything directly – with what really influenced him. And some of this is in his memoirs. He had been Foreign Secretary 20 years earlier – one of the youngest ever. His first major problem in February 1936 was Hitler's decision – a gamble as we now know – to reoccupy the Rhineland, demilitarized by the Treaty of Versailles, but a part of the German state. Lord Lothian famously described the Germans as 'only walking into their own backyard'. Nevertheless, it was an open breach of treaty unilaterally made without consultation with anyone.

It has often been argued that resolute action then would have stopped Hitler in his tracks – perhaps resulted in his removal by some sort of military *coup d'état*. Maybe or maybe not. The record of military resistance to Hitler leaves a host of question marks. But certainly in 1936 Hitler would not have risked a military confrontation with a France backed by Britain. And so the expansion of Germany via the *Anschluss* with Austria, Munich, Prague, the invasion of Poland, might not have occurred if France and Britain had stood firm over the Rhineland in 1936. However this may be, Eden believed it, and drew a parallel with events in 1956.

Here was a strident aggressive nationalist dictator with seemingly boundless ambitions in the Middle East. A dictator, moreover, like Hitler, virulently anti-Semitic, bent on driving the Jews of Israel into the sea, and bitterly anti-British with atavistic memories of the Balfour Declaration and its later effect on the pan-Arab movement which Nasser purported to lead, despite the fact that the Egyptians, as Eden, who knew the history of the Middle East very well, often pointed out, are not Arabs at all in any meaningful sense of the word.

There was no real parallel with Hitler, head of the most formidable industrial power in Europe and hence the most potentially formidable military power. Nasser was a tin-pot dictator of no great importance. In regarding it as vital to topple him (for that was what Suez was all about) Eden had learnt the wrong lesson from history.

But are there right lessons to be learnt from history? I think there are. It depends on the sort of historian you consult. I am a strong opponent of the 'inevitabilist' school of historians – those who believe that because something happened it must have happened. I believe that the inevitable is usually something which people have not tried hard enough to avoid. I am especially sceptical about those who try to project 'inevitabilism' into the future, which is no business of historians anyway. The arch-example is Karl Marx and his acolytes and followers. They laid down a predictable pattern of the future development of society. There were trends and events which economic forces were bound to create. They could not be foreseen in exact detail obviously, but the general outline could be predicted.

One of the most striking political changes between 1919 and 1939 was the growth of Fascism or authoritarian dictatorships of a very similar nature whether or not bearing that name. This occurred all over Western Europe except in Britain, and in France, where it very nearly happened, and after 1940 under Pétain, actually did. None of the Marxists or 'Marxist historians' predicted this development. The growth of fanatical nationalism did not fit in with the ideas of 'the International'. And there were practical consequences in the Marxist failure to recognize the nature of Fascism. It was explained by the Marxists that Hitler and Mussolini were ephemeral phenomena too unimportant to be mentioned in the Marxist blueprint for the future – mere bubbles on the broad stream of the inevitability towards the rule of the proletariat. In 1933, the German Communists were instructed by Stalin not to fuss about their apparently most dangerous opponents, the Nazis, who would by the laws of history disappear. The true enemy was the 'social Fascists', i.e. the Social Democrats, the German equivalent of the British Labour Party. It was an error for which the German Communists were to pay dearly, apart from those who did not quickly defect to the Nazis.

Nationalism was the principal political force in nineteenth-century Europe and South America, in twentieth-century Asia and Africa. It colours religion. Let no-one imagine that the religious feuds in Ulster have the slightest connection with belief in the Real Presence or the Seven Sacraments or Papal infallibility. They are symbols of national or perhaps, equally relevant, tribal loyalties. It colours economics. The disputes about the Euro are really disputes about national identity, not about the balance of payments or the level of interest rates.

I quote these cases not to pronounce on their merits, but merely to point out the fallibility of historical 'inevitabilism' and the uselessness of imposing a doctrinaire dogma about the past and using it to predict the future. The Liberal historians after 1919, the Leaguophiles who expected the dawn of parliamentary democracy, were equally wrong, but they did not make that dawn a decisive precursor of a sunlit high noon. They recognized that there were such things as clouds, even thunderstorms. I think that one of the most important things that history teaches us is the element of contingency and chance, bad luck and good luck, accidents of personality and events, which shape our times. It would be generally agreed that the Second World War, though it ended over fifty years ago, still affects our attitudes to a host of problems. To those of my generation – I was 22 when it broke out – it remains a subject of perpetual fascination. Not because of my own experiences at the fall of Tobruk and escaping as a POW in Italy in 1944 – a subject on which I could, but will not, discourse at much length.

No. What intrigues me about the history of the Second World War is the element of chance which led to the defeat of Hitler. And let us not forget that, if he had won we would be living, if at all, in a far worse world than we now inhabit. In other words, the war was well worth winning, and defeat, or even the compromise peace restrospectively advocated by, for example, Alan Clark *et al.*, would have been a major disaster for the civilized values of the West. Germany and Japan were defeated in the end by an alliance of the Soviet Union, America and Britain. Given the immense economic power of America and the numerical power of the USSR, it may seem inevitable that the Axis countries would succumb. But the creation of that alliance was only achieved after 1941 and its full weight was not brought to bear on Germany and Japan till 1943. Many things might have occurred earlier to frustrate such an alliance ever coming into existence.

The first turning point was the appointment of Churchill as Prime Minister in 1940. It was an unpredictable stroke of luck that in Britain, after the fall of France, there should have been a statesman able to unite the country in determination to fight on. Objectively, Britain had lost the battle. Hitler was the master of Europe thanks to the co-operation of Stalin. In the words of Hugh Trevor-Roper (Lord Dacre) who was best man at my wedding 45 years ago (so I can quote him without permission!), 'Objectively in 1940 Hitler had won the war in the West and Britain's refusal to accept defeat was illogical, unrealistic, absurd.'[3]

Churchill refused to accept this verdict. People sometimes say that he became Prime Minister by the 'will of the people'. This is nonsense. How could anyone know the 'will of the people' in 1940? The appointment was a matter of Neville Chamberlain's advice to the King. Chamberlain preferred Lord Halifax, as indeed did the King. The Tory Party preferred Lord Halifax. So did the Labour Party, though old Labourites like Barbara Castle pretend otherwise. Halifax could have had it for the asking. He refused – greatly to his credit. He was an honourable man who felt that he was not fitted for a wartime Prime Minister. And he was not sure that Britain could fight on. Had he been appointed he would almost certainly have sought the negotiated peace which was on offer. There are those who say that this would have been a good thing. I do not agree. So it was a piece of unpredictable luck that Britain had a Prime Minister who 'matched the hour' and simply refused to admit that Hitler had won the war. He played for time and in the end time gave him what he wanted, though he could never have predicted how or when. There were at least

four occasions when accident and unpredictable chance
changed the course of the Second World War:

1) The remarkable genius of the British code-breakers.
It is an extraordinary story even now not fully disclosed.
The ability to decipher German radio-intercepts was
powerfully supported by Churchill who had been deeply
involved in – and fascinated by – the world of secret
intelligence ever since his time at the Admiralty in the
First World War. The brilliant activities of the code-
breakers at Bletchley Park were an unpredictable bonus.
The Battle of Britain could otherwise have been lost. It
nearly was anyway. Likewise the Battle of the Atlantic.

2) The unexpected decision of General Franco not to
accede to Hitler's request to allow German troops into
Spain and besiege Gibraltar. Franco was part of the
Fascist community. His victory in the Civil War had
been supported by both Mussolini and Hitler with arms
and men. He might have seemed 'a soft touch', as Mussolini turned out to be with disastrous results for Italy.
If Hitler had captured Gibraltar the whole course of
the Mediterranean War would have changed. Franco's
refusal, actuated by self-interest not ideology, turned the
course of history. For a full-scale German attack on
Gibraltar would almost certainly have been as successful
as it was on Crete.

3) Another example of chance and contingency. Who
could have predicted – certainly not Hitler himself who
was greatly annoyed – that Mussolini would launch an
attack on Greece early in 1941? It was just when Hitler

had decided, without telling Mussolini, to make a massive invasion of Russia. Hitler had to back Mussolini. But the resulting delay in the attack on Russia – some two months – may have prevented a victory which very nearly came off and, if it had, would have changed the whole course of history. To quote Lord Dacre:

> Would Japan have wantonly attacked Pearl Harbor when defeated Britain and Russia offered an undefended prey? Would America have intervened in Europe when there was no bridgehead left, in order to save Communist Russia? Is it not much more likely that Hitler's dream would have been realised, that a German empire would have been established dominating Europe and much of Asia; that, in Hitler's own phrase, the German age of the world would have begun?[4]

I could add a fourth unpredictable stroke of luck for the West and this is connected with Pearl Harbor. I do not refer to the far-fetched theory that Churchill, through radio-intercepts, knew of the forthcoming Japanese assault and kept the knowledge to himself in the hope that it would bring America into the war. There has never been a shred of evidence for what is anyway a most implausible surmise. I am referring to Hitler's decision after Pearl Harbor to declare war on America. He had no need to do this. He was not even bound by treaty to do it. In any case, when was Hitler ever constrained by treaty obligations? His whole political life had been one of breaking treaties. I think that historians have somewhat neglected this decision. They certainly have not explained it. And it was one of great importance for Britain. It made possible Roosevelt's major strategic decision to give priority in the American war effort to the defeat of Hitler. Even so, this priority was not inevitable, and there were powerful quarters in Washington who wished to concentrate first on Japan. But the choice made by Roosevelt would not have been possible if Hitler had not declared war on America. Perhaps events might have led to hostilities between America and Germany, though this is not at all certain. One can safely say that the course of the war would have been very different if Hitler had been given time to perfect his V weapons, to take just one example.

I have taken these examples from the history of the Second World War to illustrate the point that there is no such thing as scientific history. You can have a history of science of course, and very good ones exist. But history is not itself a science. The political configuration of the world at any particular time is not deducible from previous history. Human error, accident, folly, incompetence are not susceptible to scientific laws. Harold Macmillan, when asked what were the worst problems for a Prime Minister, replied 'Events, dear boy, events.' And events are not predictable.

I am not saying that one can learn nothing from history. I think the Conservative party could have done so. I once wrote in a book or article that one can make a safe generalization about party (not just Conservative) political history. A united party may not always win.

But an openly divided party invariably loses. The lessons of 1906 and 1997 – the two greatest Tory disasters – confirm this law of politics, also confirmed by Labour's ruinous divisions in the 1980s. Look to the past to explain the allegedly Stalinist tendency in New Labour. I ought to add that the Tory collapse in May 1997 was not only due to divisions within. But that is another story.

And that word 'story' brings me to the end of my lecture. History can illuminate the present. I met in Peking in 1980 a young employee of Jardine Matheson who had studied mediaeval history at Oxford. He said that this was a better guide to what Communist China was really like than any contemporary studies. I would have liked to ask more but we were at what the Chinese called a banquet and further conversation drowned by endless toasts made it impossible.

But having said that history can illuminate the present, I do not believe that this is the main reason for reading it. As I said earlier, I regard such illumination as a bonus. The real point about history is that in the hands of the best writers it is a wonderful story which perpetually fascinates and stirs the imagination, like literature, art and music. That is its real justification as a study.

Notes

1. Robert Birley, *History and Idealism*, 1990
2. Lady Gwendolen Cecil, *Life of Lord Salisbury, Vol. II*, 1921 p. 38, quoting *Quarterly Review* October 1872.

3. Ed. Hugh Lloyd Jones, Valerie Pearl and Blair Worden, *History and Imagination, Essays in Honour of H. R. Trevor-Roper*, 1981, p. 360
4. Op. cit. p. 361

Seeing Ourselves:
The Scientist's Perspective

DANAH ZOHAR

When I was a child aged somewhere between five and
ten, there were two main influences, in my life: science
and religion. My grandparents, who raised me, were
simple Methodist country people who believed quite
literally in the New Testament and in all the stories
about Jesus and with them I sang those beautiful
Methodist hymns. At the same time, in my childhood,
I was decorating my bedroom with star charts and pictures of the planets and trying, even at that young age,
to put the two together. By the age of thirteen, science
won; it was then that I discovered quantum physics
and I spent all my teenage years doing 'mad scientist'
experiments in my bedroom. Also, because I discovered
quantum physics at such a young age, I found that I
was answering for myself all those big questions adoles-
cents ask about the meaning of life and my place in the
universe: Who am I? What am I here for? What does it
mean that I must die? I answered these in terms of the
things I was learning in quantum physics. Indeed, I
became very interested in the relationship between science and culture in general. On leaving high school, I
went to Massachusetts Institute of Technology (MIT),

on a physics scholarship, to train to be a physicist because I thought that's what I wanted to be. Within six months of starting at MIT I realized I absolutely detested physics and that what really had interested me all along was something that you might describe as the philosophy of physics or philosophy through physics. I was interested in the way that quantum physics had given me personally (and I thought could give culture as a whole) a new way of interpreting our experience.

The relationship between science and culture is very interesting. My view of that relationship is controversial. There are some philosophers of science who would say I am talking absolute relativist tommyrot! I believe that science and culture are inextricably linked. I believe, too, that science grows out of the wider culture, and that it is no accident that science is pretty much a Western phenomenon – indeed a Western European pheno-menon. Science has a wonderful capacity for focusing the experience of the wider culture and expressing it in striking new language. It uses powerful new metaphors, powerful images, which then go on to reflect back to that wider culture and influence it further. This is clear in Newtonian science, with its growth out of the Enlight-enment, the Protestant Reformation and the rise of rationalism. It is clear again in twentieth-century sci-ence. But to lay my cards on the table, I hold, without question, the view that it is through science that the majority of us interpret most of our experience, and I think we cannot do otherwise.

What we call Newtonian physics began in about the fifteenth century. It was finally formalized by Newton in the seventeenth century. Newtonian physics was emerging at a time when massive cultural changes were happening in Europe. At the time of the Protestant Reformation individuals were challenging the Pope and his clergy: 'Get out of our way – we don't need you. We need neither you nor your Church to stand between us and God. We as individuals will relate to God through our own capacity.' And that capacity was Reason. During the Age of Rationalism the general belief was that each human being contains the sacred gift of Reason. Through Reason, all (reasonable) human beings have direct access to the truth, and any two reasonable human beings will agree on anything because there is only one voice of Reason. Newtonian physics came along and much in the spirit of the Protestants said to the Pope, his clergy, the wise men and the stuffy old books: 'Get out of our way. We don't need you to interpret nature for us. We rational scientists will look at the data. We'll observe things; we'll measure things; we'll test things.' This tenet, which today we take so much for granted (any three-year-old already knows he must do experiments to find out why sugar dissolves in water) was radically new in the fifteenth, sixteenth and seventeenth centuries. It was the foundation of the culture in which all of us have grown up and into which we have been educated. Newton took this synthesis of current thinking within his contemporary culture and formulated it into three laws of motion. These were profoundly simple laws of motion, which caught the imagination of nearly every great thinker who was to follow in his footsteps over the next two hundred years.

Newtonian physics had certain characteristics that it's important for us to bear in mind because they will help us to understand why we have interpreted our culture through science and why we shall continue to do so. Newton argued, as did the ancient Greeks, that the world consisted of *atoms*. Each atom was a hard, impenetrable, solid, billiard-ball-like object, isolated in space and time from every other atom. Each atom related to all other atoms through forces of collision; they knocked each other off course. No atom could get inside any other atom because each atom was the smallest thing possible in the universe.

Newtonian physics was *deterministic*. On the basis of his three simple laws of motion, Newton argued that we could say anything at all about anything in the physical world. These three simple laws emerge again in the law of gravitation. Because everything was bound by law, everything was predictable, everything was certain. All the uncertainties of mediaevel life were suddenly washed away with Newtonian simplicity. Indeed, that was part of the credo of Newtonian physics: the physical world is simple; it is law-abiding, and it is controllable. B will always follow A in the same way if we know the starting position of A, and the forces acting upon it are the same. There are no surprises in Newton's universe – it's rather a dull place, in fact. Working on the universe at the beginning of time, Newton's God wound up the mechanical clock and it has just been ticking on ever after, with the exception of the fact that it is slowly running down through the law of entropy.

Newtonian science was also *reductionist*. If you want

to know something, indeed anything at all, you dissect it into its parts. Most of you probably learned some basic scientific method in junior high school. The good scientist takes what he wants to experiment upon and he isolates it from its environment. Secondly, he breaks it down into its simplest pieces and then studies those pieces in isolation in order to discern of what the whole consists. The modern version of this is that we consist, essentially, of selfish genes.

This Newtonian science, as I said, affected every major thinker who came after Newton because it was so beautifully summed up in three simple laws. Sigmund Freud, consciously and vocally, said, 'I want to be a Newtonian. I want to be the Newton of the psyche. I want to found a scientific psychology.' Newtonian atomism for Freud became the psychology of object relations. You are an object to me and I am an object to you. Freud said that love and intimacy are impossible. The commandment to love thy neighbour as thyself is the most impossible commandment ever written. How, he says, can one object ever love another object? Newtonian determinism for Freud became the doctrine that we are the prisoners of our instincts, and the prisoners of the first five years of our lives. Freud, as you know, divided the psyche into three parts – the *id*, which is the base and dark instincts of the self, the *ego*, which is the conscience and the everyday working mind, and the *superego*, which is the expectations of society and of one's parents. He had what he called the hydraulic model of the self. The poor ego is pushed up from below by the dark forces of the instincts of sex and aggression, and it is pushed down from above by the unreasonable expectations of parents and society. Thus the ego is simply a victim of all this.

Freud was the first to make popular the notion that we are victims of our experience. This has been part of psychology ever since: in behaviourism, we are just so many Pavlovian dogs who respond by salivating when bells ring. It's there, too, in the computer model of the mind – we are the 'mind machine', as Colin Blake reminds us. Like computers, we switch on and switch off, we blow our fuses, we are programmed for success or failure. It is also there, mirrored in our legal system. So many criminals don't bother to deny they committed the crime. They say: 'Yes I committed the crime but I couldn't help it. Why? Because I had an unhappy childhood, because I didn't have enough toys, because I grew up in the wrong neighbourhood, because somebody did something awful to me. So, yes, I did it but I couldn't help it.' It has been the excuse for a large escape from responsibility. The latest version of this is the very recent one, that we are genetically programmed to be the people that we are. So there is a gene for homosexuality, a gene for executive leadership, a gene for criminality and a gene for God knows what else. It's all there in our gene code and you just can't help what you become.

As a philosopher, John Locke, the founder of liberal democracy, took over the new Newtonian atomism. Locke described himself as 'the mere under-labourer of the incomparable Mr Newton'. For Locke, the atom, that indissoluble unit, became his model for the individual in society. Lockian democracy is a society where the different atoms are in space, somehow needing to avoid each other. This is the foundation of his liberalism. There is so much emphasis in liberal democracy on tolerance, giving the other person space to be different from you, and the whole notion that the public sphere has to be neutral, because if we share the public sphere with our differences we will clash and collide and there will be unavoidable tension. Adam Smith, the greatest economist of the last two hundred years, effectively the man who started the study of economics, took his model from Newton, developing his laws of the market place, his theory of the division of labour. Marx's laws of history were similarly inspired, as were Darwin's iron laws of evolution, and Frederick Taylor's laws of the company and the division of labour in management theory. All of these people consciously looked to Newton as their mentor. As a result, all of us who have grown up in Western culture, whether we ever studied any science or not, have, I think, been taught to focus our experience through the Newtonian lens. In medicine, where one learns about the living body by studying dissected corpses, we are taught that we consist of separate working parts, just like a Newtonian machine. I consist of a heart, of kidneys, of lungs, a spleen etc. and if something goes wrong with me I'll go to the relevant specialist. God help me if I have any kind of systemic or holistic disease, because Western medicine cannot cope with it.

It is the same with our education system. Western education is fragmented into specialist disciplines. I study physics, I study biology, I study history, I study poetry, I study English, but never has anyone, throughout my education, ever told me that reading literature will make me a better physicist, that knowing some poetry will inspire my mathematics, or that knowing fine art will help my architecture and so on. We parcel up academic disciplines into fragments. We fragment and isolate ourselves into lonely unions and now more recently also into nuclear families. So our experience has been largely that of Newtonian atomism, determinism and reductionism.

At the end of the nineteenth century/beginning of the twentieth century there was a further dramatic shift in culture. It was most forcefully stated by the German philosopher Friedrich Nietzsche who argued in *Also Sprach Zarathustra* that 'God is dead'. In arguing this Nietzsche was not just making a religious statement. When Nietzsche argued that God is dead, he was saying the framework is dead – the whole paradigm through which we have found our motivation and our inspiration is dead. We are in some kind of new ball game. At the same time that Nietzsche was saying this, European art was similarly going through a massive transformation. Simple representational art, which depicted solid geometrical objects in absolute space/time frameworks, was giving way to impressionist art, abstract art. The single point of view, using Newtonian absolute space/time frameworks, was giving way to multiple perspective art. We have all seen pictures of those wonderful Picasso women with their faces pointing in many directions simultaneously.

During this same period, the First World War destroyed many of the long-held certainties about civilized behaviour in warfare and the things that civilized people would get up to in general. It raised new limits, too, to the carnage that warfare could cause. Come the twenties and thirties and we had a whole school of Existentialist philosophers saying, 'Objectivity is bad. Objectivity is impossible. Everything is subjective.' So, in the first half of this century, both through experience and through intellectual life, there was a slow unravelling of all the old certainties. It was into this intellectual climate that, in 1905, Albert Einstein announced that there are *relative* frames of reference – that there are as many space/time frames of reference as there are observers. There is no one absolute space/time frame of reference. Diversity had come into science. It was also within this same climate that the German physicist Werner Heisenberg wrote his *uncertainty* theory. 'Uncertainty,' he argued, 'is the basis of all that science will teach us in the future.' Not knowing becomes the key to knowing – there evolved a radical shift in the scientific perspective.

Through the cultural impact of this intellectual shift of focus, most of us might now agree, from our personal experience, that this is the age of uncertainty, the age of ambiguity – some might even call it the age of confusion. The historian Eric Hobsbawm has called it the *Age of Extremes*. In the book of that title he argues that there has been more change in the last fifty years than since the Stone Age. The old verities no longer hold very well. Science is blamed for much of this. I am not convinced myself that the content of science has had much to do with the rise of the age of uncertainty and the age of ambiguity. I cannot agree with those theologians and historians of religion who believe that, because science makes it seem doubtful there can be miracles, we cannot believe in the virgin birth, or that because science makes it impossible to believe that any dead body could become alive again, therefore the Resurrection could not have happened. This does not seem to me to be really important. Instead, I believe that science has made a major change to religion, because the *spirit* of science has made a major change to religion. The actual content of Newtonian science was rather like the old religion. Scientific method and objective observation, which looked for laws and principles, were not very different from the laws carved in stone that came down to us from Sinai.

The scientific spirit is very different from the content of Newtonian science. The scientific spirit is about exploration – it is about falsifiability; it is about living on the edge; it is about looking for patterns rather than for laws and principles; it is about doing experiments and it is about taking risks. Twentieth-century science no longer feels that science has to be pinned on certainty, on iron-clad laws and principles, because it knows that these are all of limited use. They are applicable if you want to build a bridge; they are applicable if you want to put a man on the moon. There is nothing wrong with Newton's physics. It is just that today we know that Newton's physics is a small band of experience within the much larger band of experience that science can describe. Inevitably, since we are only five minutes into the history of the universe, our science will change. But the scientific spirit, I think, will not change. It is a spirit which says, 'Any truth has to stand the test of falsifiability.' I must always be prepared, where experiments show it to be necessary, to accept that my theory of today will be replaced by another theory tomorrow. I must always be humble. Science has such a reputation for arrogance and there are certainly many arrogant scientists about; they are not good scientists. A good scientist cannot help but be humble. A good scientist knows that anything he knows today may be overtaken by tomorrow's discovery and he holds himself ready for that. He celebrates being proved wrong.

In my books and other writings, when I talk about the new science of the twentieth century I talk mostly of quantum physics. There are in fact four new sciences this century. There is *relativity theory*, Einstein's work, which is about huge distances and very fast speeds. There is *quantum physics*, which began as a study of the very small, the world within the atom – the word 'quantum' itself means the smallest unit of action possible in the world. And then in the sixties we saw the birth of two new sciences, or quasi-sciences – nobody is quite sure whether they rank quite fully as sciences yet – which are the *chaos theory* and *complexity science*. Philosophers of science generally agree that, of the four, quantum theory is the most philosophically fundamental. It is quantum theory that challenges our way of looking at things. It is quantum theory that challenges the very ethos of science – not the *scientific spirit*, but the content and ethos of Newtonian science.

When Newtonian physics argues that the world consists of separate atoms each isolated in its own place in space and time, quantum physics teaches us that the world consists not of atoms but of patterns of dynamic energy. Each of us, each existing thing in this universe, from a quantum upward, is a pattern of dynamic energy. These patterns of dynamic energy have particle-like aspects which are localizable, measurable, touchable, pin-downable. Each quantum event also has a wave-like aspect, a potentiality to be different things, and the wave-like aspects of every quantum constituent in the universe overlap with those of every other. Holism has replaced atomism in twentieth-century science. 'There is no such thing as separateness,' wrote the scientist and philosopher David Baum. 'Separateness is an illusion.' Everything in the universe is interwoven like the strands of a carpet. Even more dramatically so because in quantum holism, even the very identity of the individual constituent, whether the constituent is me as a human being, or a speck of dust or an atom, is caught up into relationship with the other things and so is defined through its relationships. So there is no atomless isolation as in the old physics.

Quantum physics, as one might guess from the term 'the uncertainty principle', is radically free. It is indeterministic rather than deterministic. You don't know why or when or how a single quantum event might happen, or how it got to where it is, or where it is going to. If you have a million quantum events you can construct from them a probability distribution curve and then predict how another million will generate another pattern like that. But a single quantum event is a radically free agent. You cannot predict it. The old science told us that there was a split between the human subject, the scientist and that which he observes, i.e. a split between the observer and the observed. A good Newtonian scientist stands outside his experiment. Objectivity is the name of the game in Newtonian science, and it has become a cultural value. You must be objective. Therefore the detached expert is more likely to see the situation more clearly than a member of the group. The new science tells us that this is impossible. In quantum physics you simply cannot separate the observer from what he observes. In the quantum holism, where everything is identified through its relationships, I, the observer, am inside the system. The experimental apparatus I design will affect the outcome of my experiment.

There was a very famous experiment in quantum physics which sought to discern whether light is *wave* light or *particle* light. In the nineteenth century, scientists were confused about this since some of their experiments showed light to be a series of electrons moving like little particles along wires, whereas other experiments showed the light to be like waves in a waterpool. They could not decide between waves and particles. Well, quantum physics came along and said: 'You people are asking the wrong question. It is not either/or, it is both/and.' Here is another distinction between the two sciences. In the most famous experiment, I think, in quantum physics, called the 'two slit experiment', a means was devised to observe this phenomenon. The scientists found that if you have a source of light over here, and then you have an opaque barrier with two slits in it, you can ask light two questions. If you ask light the question, 'Are you particle light? There are some particle detectors here.' Lo and behold, the light comes through one slit and goes 'click, click, click, click' and says, 'Yes, I am a stream of particles.' On the other hand, if you say to light, 'Are you a wave?' and you ask this question by putting a screen by the barrier, light comes through both the slits in interfering waves and builds up an interference pattern on the screen. There is no way you can do this experiment to catch light in this double screen. There is no way you can do this experiment to catch light in this double act. The question you ask determines the answer you get. In 'quantum physics philosophy' this is called living in a participatory universe. We are not objective outsiders in an alien universe, as Jacques Monod called it, nor strangers in an alien reality, or something like that. In quantum philosophy and quantum physics we are evolutionary agents. We hope to make reality happen – we live in a participative universe.

One of the great problems for us today is to know how to put together the ethical dilemmas within which we have been caught – the sense of loss, the ambiguity, the uncertainty which affects our ethical lives. It affects our community, individuals, global business. It results from the death of the old religion, or at least the greatly diminished influence of the old religion, and the rise of science. There is no sensible way, or at least no such powerful a way, of broaching the problem of how to arrive at a new ethics of our time, except through what this new science is telling us about the universe and ourselves. To have a theory of ethics today we need a theory of precursing – we need to know who we are, where we come from, how we fit in, how we belong. It is, after all, science that answers these questions for us. And there are two very conflicting messages coming from science because very few people make a distinction between the Newtonian science of the seventeenth, eighteenth and nineteenth centuries, and the new science of the twentieth century. I would argue that the old Newtonian science is very anti-ethical. For instance, look at the notion of determinism: I am not responsible, I am not a free agent, because I am determined by iron laws of the universe, or because I am determined by my genes, because I am determined by my experience. It is very hard to found an ethics on that. This has led to some of the ethical defeatism that many people feel. Talking with a group of management people, I remember a young man in the group saying: 'I don't see why you're talking about the meaning of life. Life clearly has no meaning and what's the point?' He went on to describe us as 'simple carbon units'. In the rest of his comments, he equally discounted ethics, motivation, vision, value and everything else that we hold dear to humanity.

On another occasion, I attended a series of lectures at an Oxford church. It was a series of evening group meetings for people whom the vicar called religious doubters, that is people who were having just a little bit of trouble with what they were hearing from the pulpit on Sunday morning. At one of these meetings, a young woman said very despairingly: 'Well, now that science has proven to us that God doesn't exist, it just doesn't matter how we behave, because it's just up to us.' And being just up to us, for her, meant it's down to nothing, to a bunch of carbon units, to selfish genes, to all the things that science had told her about herself. I think that we desperately need a new ethics of personal responsibility founded in a wiser, deeper, more scientific understanding of the nature of the person, and that through this we shall have the basis for a most amazing and relevant new vision of ethics. Let me illustrate what I mean:

If we are to produce an ethics of personal responsibility, an ethics based here with me – where I take responsibility, in which I say the buck stops here – then I am the agent who has to make things happen. As Jung put it in *The Psychology of Modern Man*, everything in the universe happens around the individual. The individual is not just the passive listener of his age. Each of us makes the age that we live in; the notion is that the individual is the centre. Now when you hear things like that they can be greatly misunderstood, because 'individual' in Newtonian psychology and Freudian psychology has meant a petty, narrow, limited ego-self. Jung did not mean anything like that by the person or by the individual. He had a concept of the larger Self, which he capitalized with an S, and which he talked about as that collective unconscious, that collective experience of all humanity, which was also intertwined with all of life on the planet and possibly even of all cosmic and physical life. Jung was quite mystical in many ways. It is that Self, that larger union Self, that I call the quantum self in my book of the same name. I too do not think we can get to a useful definition of the person, or the individual, by talking about an isolated limited thing like a petty-driven, selfish, ego-bound self. But quantum physics tells us that the self cannot be like that. Quantum physics tells us that the self is naturally part of the larger scheme of things, because everything is interwoven. We are just one of many ripples in this vast pattern of ripples that make up the universe. In quantum physics there is a theory called nominal causality. This theory argues that there can be action in the absence of local causes, so that you can have effects felt across the universe by a small thing happening elsewhere. Something very similar to this occurs in chaos theory through the so-called butterfly effect; chaos theory argues that if a butterfly flaps its wings in Beijing it can cause a tornado on the other side of the world in Kansas City. The old physics used to say that it took a very large cause to have a very large effect. The new science shows that the most tiny, infinitesimal perturbance can have a gigantic effect.

This also has a bearing, I think, on the role of the individual in the moral world. Anyway, if we are to have a new ethics of personal responsibility, we do have to have a sense that we are part of a larger scheme of things, that it is not just us here, that we are not the top of evolution's tree, that we are not the last word in evolutionary development. I said earlier that we are only five minutes into the history of the universe. I suspect most of us here would be unhappy if intelligent life was not going to evolve any further than ourselves in future years. To have an ethics of personal responsibility we also need a sense that we belong – that we are not aliens on the edge of an alien universe. The universe does not consist of iron laws of material being, with us as immaterial souls that came from God knows where, or made of God knows what, but certainly do not obey the rest of the laws of the universe. Good science would make us believe this is probably not true. At the same time, good science would not therefore, as Newtonian science does, reduce us to just our genes, to just our livers and kidneys, to just the blitz of electrical activity in our brains. Good science would say there is a lot more to be known. Good science argues that ultimately everything can be couched in scientific theories and principles, but that science itself is just a baby. Science has a lot to learn and we do not yet know how consciousness gets into the scheme of things. But we have faith that there will one day be a physics of consciousness, which will explain our higher aspirations, our higher thoughts, our sense of beauty, our sense of humour, and things like that. We need to have an ethics of personal responsibility, a notion that we are responsible. I showed how in the old physics we were not responsible, and in Freudian psychology and behaviourism we were not responsible. In the notion of the participative universe, each of us is responsible for the cold evolution of reality and the fact that we are inside creators gives us a tremendous responsibility. Part of the universe exists because I am here. Part of the universe manifests itself because of the questions I ask. Some of reality is due to me and to each and every other one of us, to each sentient being on the planet, for all we know, even down to the stones. For we do not yet know whether stones can be conscious since we do not know enough about consciousness. We cannot really say where the boundaries of consciousness stop.

I have done a little Latin research on the word 're-sponsibility'. It will not surprise you to hear that the word 'response' is directly related to it. To be responsible is to be responsive, to know that I am part of a larger system, a larger whole, and to be able to respond to the other as someone who is part of me, who is relevant to me, who is my business. In Freudian psychology, love and intimacy are impossible; I cannot love my neighbour as myself because we are all just objects. In quantum psychology you would say quite the opposite – you would say it is impossible not to love my neighbour if I love myself, because my neighbour is myself. We are all intertwined. Anyway, part of the ethics of personal responsibility is becoming more responsive and I think (though I guess it's slightly controversial to raise this because I am told one third of the nation did not feel as I did because two-thirds did) that all that was happening about Princess Diana's death was bringing to the fore how much people valued what was held to be her responsiveness – that she did not relate through codes of laws and tablets of stone, she related from the heart. She simply responded to people's needs and people's pains. So much of our ethics prior to this century has been an ethics of rules and principles and ethics of codes, beginning with Moses bringing the *big ten* down from Sinai. Jews think there are 630 of these commandments, although Gentiles only have to observe the big ten. It is those rules and codes which have been called into question by the spirit of science. So I think we need a new ethics of value and response. That response is related to responsibility did not surprise me. Another idea occurred to me, which I took to the Latin master of the school where my son is a student. I said to him: 'Isn't it possible that spontaneity is related to responsibility and response?' I was inspired to ask this question again by Diana. One of the things that I valued about her, and one of the things the commentators were saying so many people valued about her, or at least about her 'myth', was her spontaneity. She did not think twice – she said what she thought – she did what she liked doing. If she wanted to touch an AIDS patient she did. She did not care about where flags were posted on masts and protocol and all those things, and I thought it would be very nice if I could also show that in the original Latin, spontaneity was related to responsibility and response. The Latin master at first told me, 'No – it's a nice idea, but you're completely wrong.' But then he phoned me back about six hours later and said, 'Well, you're right after all.' If you go back to the earliest Latin, to be spontaneous is to be responsive/is to be responsible.

This, I think, has a very strong ethical message for us, which makes sense if interpreted by way of what science is telling us about ourselves. We are free beings, we are free agents, we are not determined and therefore we are capable of being responsive. A deterministic system cannot respond to anything – it is programmed.

We are responsible; therefore, because we are responsible we are spontaneous and responsive. Just one more interesting thing, which is something of an aside, but it is connected with this. I often wonder about good and evil – I suppose most of us do. I am writing a book at the moment, *South of the Edge*, which is trying to define the origins of good and evil. I cannot myself believe from anything I know in science, or anything I am reading in science, that human beings or any other living creatures are born with original sin. I cannot see anything that somehow corrupts us from the word go. You look at a little baby, you look at how babies come into the world, with hardly any neural connections wired up, only an open capacity for experience, and it's hard to believe that evil is programmed into us. So I have been looking for some way to account for evil where evil is something that we develop or which happens to us, but which is not original, not a force in the universe. I have been doing some Hebrew derivation. In Hebrew the devil is called Shetara, and the word Shetara, which has the same three-letter root, means unresponsiveness. And so the devil is the source of unresponsiveness. This, of course, has a powerful resonance with what I was saying about ethics being based on being responsive. A capacity for good is based on a capacity for being responsive and those people who do the most evil acts are often quite cold toward their victims. They do not seem to have a sense of the harm they are doing. They simply do not relate – they do not respond.

Finally, I believe that, if we are going to have a new ethics, indeed a new spiritual vision of any sort, we need to have some sense that there is in this universe a source of vision and value, a source of inspiration that does somehow drive our basic visions and perhaps even our basic instincts. If the universe is, as Newton described it, just a lot of dead lifeless matter, and we are somehow lost amongst this dead lifeless matter, without the old-fashioned notion of a God outside this system, it is very hard to see how we could possibly find any source of vision and value in the universe; indeed, people like Richard Dawkins and Peter Aktins argue that there is none. We are just a pool of selfish genes desperately and blindly seeking replication, with no particular rhyme or reason to what we are doing. Evolution, they say, is blind. I do not think that the new science holds that, and I shall mention something from quantum physics that gives me the basis to interpret our experience quite differently.

I told you earlier that in quantum physics every exist-ing thing, every small thing, a house or a mountain, is seen as a pattern of dynamic energy. This raises the question in a good scientist's mind, 'Well, if it's a pattern of dynamic energy that's sort of waving, what is it wav-ing on?' Electro-magnetic waves wave in an electro-magnetic field and water waves wave on the surface of water. Are they waving on or in? Quantum physics has an answer to that. It is called the quantum vacuum. In this science of energy the quantum vacuum is the lowest ground state of energy in the universe. Because it is the ground state it is not excited, it is not dynamic, it is not perturbed, it is not waving. That is why they call it the vacuum, because in quantum physics anything that exists (originally from the Latin 'to stand out from') is standing out from the vacuum by being excited. Therefore the vacuum has no qualities that we can see, or touch, or measure, because it is not excited, it does not exist. It is secure in itself. If you were looking for a God within physics or a source of vision and value within physics, the quantum vacuum would be it. A physicist would never call it God because physicists do not talk about God when they are being physicists. But the quantum vacuum is literally, just in physics terms, the source of the universe. Everything that exists in this world is an excitation of that ground state of energy which permeates the whole cosmos – it is not down there, it is not up here, it is everywhere. We are written on the vacuum like waves riding on a pond.

Since we exist, since our sense of good exists, since our sense of beauty exists, and since our aspirations exist, I want to hold as a physicist that the vacuum has got to contain these things, because otherwise how did they get here? This goes with my scientific interpretation of the universe, so I think that, given the quantum vacuum's relation to the rest of the physical universe in quantum physics, that it is only a small step, and again one that will happen more when we understand more how consciousness fits into physics, that the quantum vacuum is indeed the source of everything. Being related as excitations on the vacuum is how we are all interrelated holistically.

Each of us is, then, if you like, an agent of this unfolding universal vision of potentiality. Each of us is a wave on the sea, and you cannot, as with any wave on the sea, make any boundary between any waves on the sea. Where does one stop and the other begin? Any scientist will agree that each of us contains within ourselves the whole history of evolution in this universe. Our bodies are made out of stardust. Our minds operate by the same laws and principles as everything else in this cosmos. We are all part of the cosmos. Each of us contains within our brains the whole ecological evolution of things on the planet. Each of us thinks with the brain of the amoeba, of the frog, the cat, the monkey, the tiger, and we use them all when we think. This is one reason they are not able to make computers think like we do. We're wonderfully complex because we're wonderfully messy. We contain all the experiments, all the mistakes, all the successes that nature has turned up in these billions of years of evolution so far. So, I think, in this looking for a new spirituality, a new interpretation of ethics from the point of view of science, you would see that we are agents of the vacuum, as agents of the source of the universe, agents of the vision of the universe, which ties up with the responsibility in the sense of 'the buck stops here'. What I do, what I say, does count.

Basically, what I want to say about the old science and the new is that I do not see how one can talk about these ethical questions without referring to science. I suspect that even those who disagree with that would at least agree that you cannot approach such questions and fly against science. Science at least knows what it is talking about in what it has said so far. I want to argue that today, if one is looking for a way to make sense of oneself as a person, as a human being, if one wishes to make sense of relationships, to make sense of our social patterns, to make sense of our corporate patterns, to get some vision of how we can fulfil our potentiality, I just do not see that one can possibly look elsewhere, or at least anywhere better, than science to do it. Historians have been influenced by science in their thinking simply because science does not just give us these notions of determinism and reductionism – it gives us the very categories of thought, it gives us our paradigm, our most deeply held unconscious set of assumptions. Since the fifteenth century this unconscious set of assumptions has come from science. It permeates everything that we think about. So I rest my case.

Seeing Ourselves:
A Mirror of Eternity

JOHN HABGOOD

I am grateful for this opportunity to celebrate Launcelot Fleming's memory. I knew him as a friend, one among thousands of his friends, for he was a man who seemed to gather friends wherever he went, and for whom people were enormously important. I knew him too as an engaging, conscientious and humble man, diffident about his own abilities, despite his achievements and the range of his knowledge. It was fairly typical of him that once, when he was Dean of Windsor and I was at a conference there, he came up to me, all agitated, grabbed my arm, and said, 'John, I am desperate about my Christmas sermon; I can't think of anything fresh to say.'

'Have you tried the parable of the Good Samaritan?' I replied.

'What has that got to do with it?'

'It has the clearest description of the meaning of the incarnation in only six words.'

'What words?'

'The Samaritan came where he was.'

He immediately got the point. The priest and the Levite may have been good men, deeply committed to their religion, but they went by on the other side of the road. The Samaritan, the despised and rejected one, saw the wounded man, and 'came where he was'. That is indeed what Christmas is about.

Launcelot thanked me and preached the sermon, and to his credit wrote to me about it afterwards. I tell the story because the parable also seems to fit so perfectly the character of his own ministry. Friendship is about being where people are, interrupting our own journey, if need be, in order to be with them, and accompanying them on their way. Launcelot took endless trouble with people, and those who enjoyed his friendship knew from the constant stream of letters that they were never forgotten.

One of the gifts of friendship is to enable people to see themselves more clearly and to value themselves more highly, as their image is reflected in a true friend's concern for them. Friendship is not just a question of liking people, but includes seeing and valuing in them capacities which they perhaps can't yet believe in. Such concern can be both humbling and reassuring. We can face the worst in ourselves if we can be confident that we are not going to be rejected. And we can see greater possibilities in ourselves if we know that someone else believes in us. This is the essence of pastoral ministry, and it is the human counterpart of the grace of God. At the heart of Christian theology is the belief that in some sense God himself accompanies us in friendship, and that we come to know ourselves more truly, as we see our own reflection in the light of his presence and under the assurance of his love.

If, therefore, we are to see ourselves and our contemporary society from a theological perspective, as my instructions for this lecture require, this is one way of setting about it. We can focus on the discomfiting and reassuring awareness of God's concern for us, the God who will not let us go, but comes where we are, even to the place where all seems lost in death; and we can hope to see, in his eternal concern for us, a reflection of ourselves and our world. Hence my title, 'A Mirror of Eternity'.

But unfortunately this business of reflection is not quite as straightforward as that. Mirrors, where they are mentioned at all in the Bible, are as much a source of frustration as of illumination, doubtless because in those days they were not very effective. Paul, writing to the Corinthians, who made mirrors, contrasts seeing in a mirror and seeing directly. 'Now we see in a glass darkly, but then face to face' (1 Corinthians 13). 'Darkly' because just as mirrors were bad, so the vision of God is enigmatic. One day we shall know, even as we are known. But here on earth we have only what the Revised English Bible translates as 'puzzling reflections in a mirror'. Theology needs to start with the reminder that it is always partial and provisional.

St James in his epistle is even more dismissive of mirrors. Reflected images were, to him, not only secondary to the actual business of living the gospel, but also, like much theology, eminently forgettable. 'Anyone who listens to the message but does not act on it is like somebody looking in a mirror at the face nature gave him; he glances at himself and goes his way, and promptly forgets what he looked like.'

Do we forget? Not those of us who every morning laboriously take our faces off or put them on, and who know every bump and wrinkle. It is quite hard to think oneself back into a world in which mirrors were such poor reflectors, and so rare that most people had only the vaguest idea of what they really looked like. Ancient glass was coarse in texture and semi-opaque. Only in the thirteenth century did the Venetian glassmakers invent a glass which was tough enough and transparent enough to make lenses, proper stained-glass windows and silver-backed mirrors. The way was open for people to gain a new understanding of the universe, a new pictorial image of Scripture, and a new view of themselves. People became more conscious of their appearance, and more interested in matching their faces to their thoughts. While the new lenses gradually revealed a universe of infinite space, seemingly empty of God, the new mirrors were focusing attention on the individual and on the inner life as the touchstone of reality. Thus glass technology took its place as the unlikely catalyst of one of the many revolutions which have created our contemporary world. It is a world in which we are inordinately interested in ourselves, and in which the preferred route to God, if he is sought at all, is to look inward to the depths of the self. Indeed, I have started this lecture on the basis of this very presupposition, that learning to know God has its counterpart in self-discovery.

Before pursuing this point, however, I want to look briefly at the wider social scene, where the effects of this preoccupation with ourselves are now all too evident. About a year ago I was asked to review a book called

Holding up a Mirror sub-titled *How Civilisations Decline*. It is an ambitious 650-pager, written by an elderly lady in Devon, who had tried to pack it with a lifetime's learning. I do not think it will be widely read. But the central thesis is interesting and worth rescuing from oblivion. The 'mirror' of the title is the theatre, and the author's aim was to illustrate how changes in the character of the theatre in different periods have reflected the moral state of society. For instance, the decline from the classic age of Greek theatre into pantomime and pornography, mirrored the decline of Greek civilization. The same was true of Rome, where the theatre lost its original moral seriousness and, as the Empire disintegrated, became obsessed with brutality and spectacle. One might say the same of our own age, in which much of what passes for entertainment seems to have lost its moral bearings; indeed, a substantial part of the book is a long catalogue of moans about the state of society as revealed by the media. But what makes it worth mentioning in this context is its use of the work of a little-known Russian sociologist named Sorokin. Sorokin was born and educated in pre-revolutionary Russia, escaped in 1922, and eventually became Professor of Sociology at Harvard. His *magnum opus* was published just before the Second World War, was documented by an enormous research team, was so detailed as to be almost unreadable, and sank without a trace when the war turned attention elsewhere.

But the admirable Miss Glyn-Jones *has* read him, and taken on board his encyclopaedic theory about three types of society. Sorokin distinguished between what he called 'ideational' societies, 'idealist' ones, and 'sensate' ones. *Ideational* societies are other-worldly; reality lies in the soul; religion is a primary feature of everyday life; and guidance lies in the hands of the priests and the prophets. A range of societies from ancient tribalism to modern Iran fall into this category. An *idealist* society is more relaxed about religion and is sensitive towards material aspirations, while not allowing material interests to dictate values. Ideals and values inform, but do not dominate, everyday life. Classical Greece, Republican Rome and to some extent Victorian Britain, were mainly idealist. A *sensate* society has marginalized its religion and its ideals; it relies on the senses, as the sources of pleasure, as the arbiters of what is true and as the basis of values. Imperial Rome, late mediaeval Europe, England in the Restoration period, and much of late twentieth-century Western civilization, can all be described as more or less sensate.

Much of Sorokin's primary material came from his experience in Russia during the transition to communism, and he saw at first hand what happens to a society when its people lose any sense of values which transcend their own immediate desires for self-fulfilment. Let me give you one quote from him – I suspect an uncharacteristically readable one:

> If a person has no strong convictions as to what is right and what is wrong, if he does not believe in God or absolute moral values, if he no longer respects contractual obligations, and finally, if his hunger for pleasure and sensory values is paramount, what can

guide and control his conduct towards other men? Nothing but his desires and lusts. Under these conditions he loses all rational and moral control, even plain common sense. What can deter him from violating the rights, interests, and well-being of other men? Nothing but physical force. How far will he go in his insatiable quest for sensory happiness? He will go as far as brute force, opposed by that of others, permits. His whole problem of behaviour is determined by the ratio between his force and that wielded by others.[1]

That may seem exaggerated and alarmist, until one remembers the number of societies and nations in today's world, most obviously in Africa, which are facing precisely this dilemma because their moral framework has collapsed, just as Sorokin experienced it in revolutionary Russia. And we can see examples, too, of the reactions provoked when such collapse is feared, as in the kind of ideational society the Moral Majority tried to imposed on the United States, and which Taleban has imposed on parts of Afghanistan. If force is the only way of bringing order to a society, then force will be used; and if reform has an ideological component, then morals backed by sanctions are likely to be part of the package. Exaggerated or not, I believe extreme examples of this kind expose the dilemma of modern societies which rightly want to maximize freedom, but lack the moral or spiritual basis for exercising it without disaster. One doesn't have to sign up to Sorokin's theory to see that societies can be characterized by the priority they give to ideas, beliefs and values. When these are lacking, there is a slide towards disintegration. When they have become too dominant, there is the repressive use of force. The ever-increasing volume of legislation in modern societies is an ominous symptom. People are losing the habit of what has, rather tellingly, been called 'obedience to the unenforceable'. There is a reliance on law to make up for the decline of public morals, but it is a hopeless task. The assumptions and attitudes of mind which legislation cannot touch, are in reality the most crucial determinants of the quality of a society.

All this has repercussions on the way we understand ourselves. One might use Sorokin's analysis back-to-front by observing how the kind of self-discovery facilitated by a particular culture depends on the beliefs, or lack of them, which are presupposed by it. If it is true that ours is becoming a more and more sensate society, then it is not surprising if self-discovery increasingly takes the form of stimulation or gratification of the senses. The drug culture is an obvious example. Happiness comes out of a bottle, or syringe, or pipe, or pill. Other people may look for self-discovery through physical stress, as in dangerous sports. I suppose you can learn quite a lot about yourself through bungee jumping, but I am not going to try. And then there are the various kinds of extremism designed to shock, as in the arts and even nowadays in the Royal Academy (very sensate), or in the spectacle of vicarious destruction and cruelty in the cinema and on television. The possibility that ideas might be more significant than sensual experience, or that the spiritual explorers of the past might still have something to teach us, seems to many of our contemporaries, if not incomprehensible, at least profoundly boring. 'Be real,' they say. In a sensate society the priority lies with individual feeling and experience.

In the second of Sorokin's types, the well-balanced idealistic society, self-discovery begins with what is outside us – a world to explore, and a given set of values with which to explore it. Thus friendship, to return to my main theme, can deepen our self-understanding and self-acceptance, because our friends are other than ourselves, and represent values outside us. Provided they are not there simply to gratify us, they can act as a mirror in which we learn to see more of the truth about ourselves.

In Christian tradition, the presence of the God who comes where we are, acts as a more perfect mirror than our always imperfect friends. In more general terms, I want to claim that belief in a divine reality, as other than and prior to us, has been one of the factors shaping the development of human personality. It is no coincidence that religion seems to have been the matrix out of which a distinctively human culture was formed. When the Bible speaks of man being made in the image of God, this can be read as a more succinct way of making the same point. Nowadays, of course, we are more aware than previous generations that the traffic did not all flow in one direction. There are plenty of instances in all religions, including biblical religion, of God being made in the image of man, and that is why he is sometimes presented as doing such terrible things.

But no imagery would have developed at all without some perception that what was happening was inter-action, rather than invention. I am fond of a quotation from Austin Farrer which beautifully expresses what such interaction might entail. He is writing about the origin of the idea of kingship in the OT:

> When human kings arose, invisible divine kings stood behind their thrones. Indeed, kingship worthy of the name is distinguished from mere leadership by the divinity which supports it. Now, if kings arose with divine support, we might suppose that the divine king was already known: for how can the human king be clothed with divine authority except by a divine king already acknowledged? But then, on the other hand, until men have seen human kings, how can they know what a divine king would be? In fact, the human king and his divine archetype arise at once, they are inseparable: each makes the other.[2]

This refinement of imagery by mutual interaction could apply equally well to the presence of the One who comes where we are, thereby acting as the mirror in which we can see ourselves more fully. We might adapt Farrer's analogy, for instance, and ask whether human beings need some parallel inkling of divine transcendence, in order to shape and develop our own capacity for self-transcendence. What could be the content of our frustrated yearnings to transcend ourselves, without some concept, however vague, of that which is higher than ourselves? Or again if, at the purely human level, each of us develops as a person through our interaction with other persons, is there anything in the sum of these interactions which corresponds with the oneness we discern within ourselves? Is there some over-arching personal reality in relation to which our own identity can be known? Or if we think in terms of the historical revelation of God's being and activity, isn't there also a sense in which this can be interpreted as a process of human self-discovery? When the Psalmist says of idols, 'They that make them are like unto them,' he is expressing a travestied version of the same insight. We become like what we worship.

In a society where beliefs about God are held to be supremely important, it is not hard to see how divine revelation and human self-discovery might have complemented one another. But in a sensate society the priority is different. The starting point is not an awareness of being in relationship with the transcendent reality against which our life is measured, and in the presence of which we grow as persons. The starting point is simply the evidence of our own senses, stripped of any awareness of a personal or transcendent other. This concentration on the senses may lead to anything from sober scientific materialism which excludes the personal, to unbridled self-centred hedonism which identifies the personal with the sensual. Awareness of relationship with the other becomes secondary, a matter of deduction or exploitation, rather than direct encounter. Thus materialism and hedonism are both, in their different ways, examples of walking by on the other side of the road. The other is an object to be viewed, not a person to be met. And instead of self-discovery being seen as in some sense a response to the God who meets us in the other, he is regarded, if he is considered at all, as at best an object of interest, a possible adjunct to human fulfilment, and at worst as an obstacle.

This may seem a very abstract analysis, so let me try to put some flesh on it by describing two forms of self-understanding which nowadays receive a lot of publicity, though I suspect they are still fairly untypical. I have in mind the autonomous self and the post-modern, or deconstructed self. They are obviously extreme types, but they can serve as markers when we turn to the question of how theology, in this sort of context, can enable us to see ourselves differently.

Beliefs about the autonomous self began to take hold during the Enlightenment, as part of the shift I have been describing. Instead of starting from God as the foundation of knowledge, philosophy started from Descartes' awareness of himself. 'I think, therefore I am.' And this starting point was soon seen to have moral implications, too. Insofar as we are rational individuals, so the argument goes, we are responsible only to ourselves. The law of our being is within us; that is what autonomy means. Shakespeare said it first, through Polonius: 'to thine own self be true'. Mere obedience, particularly obedience to arbitrary law forbidding the knowledge of good and evil, is a craven virtue. Indeed, the notion that humanity's original sin was disobedience, looks distinctly jaded beside the achievements which have sprung from human curiosity and self-assertion. The freedom to be ourselves is fundamental to our humanity, and two centuries of struggle to emancipate one group after another have elevated autonomy to a primary goal. Even in medicine, once the most paternalistic of professions, patient autonomy is now more or less taken for granted.

But autonomy can take various forms. There is the weak autonomy of those who are not in revolt against anything much, but just want space in which to live their own lives. Autonomy can be valued alongside the recognition that there have to be limits to it, if the autonomy of others is not to be compromised. Religion may be tolerated, or even welcomed, by those who see God as helping them to fulfil what are essentially their own goals.

There is also a strong, much more self-assertive, autonomy, which *is* in revolt, and which in its origins was predominantly a revolt against religion. Nietzsche is the obvious example, with his supreme contempt for what he saw as the slave morality of Christianity. One quotation must suffice: '*if* there were gods, how could I endure not to be a god! *Therefore* there are no gods.'[3] There are not many Nietzsches, but there are plenty of people today who would rather not believe in God, because they see belief as essentially restrictive, rather than empowering. The constant image of religion in much popular writing today is that it is narrow, moralistic and interfering. What I have said about the presence of the God who comes where we are, cuts no ice because, for a variety of reasons, no doubt some of them personal, even the friendship of God can feel restrictive. God is seen as the enemy of autonomy, not the one who sets us free to be our true selves. To modern autonomous man, John Donne's great sonnet must seem absurd.

Batter my heart, three person'd God; for you
As yet but knock, breathe, shine and seek to mend;
That I may rise, and stand, o'erthrow me, and bend
Your force, to break, blow, burn and make me new.
. . .

Take me to you, imprison me, for I
Except you enthrall me, never shall be free,
Nor ever chaste, except you ravish me.

The Christian belief that one has to lose one's life in order to find it, is the complete antithesis to the claims of strong self-assertive autonomy. It particularly enrages those who, like some feminists, believe that they have lost enough of life already, and who see self-assertive autonomy as a characteristically masculine failing anyway. But it is ironic that frequently those who are most fiercely self-sufficient are also the ones who are most acutely aware of the longing for some form of self-transcendence, albeit by self-assertion. And how do they seek it? As we have seen, they often seek it by deliberately courting danger; by climbing mountains, or sailing round the world, or risking everything to build up a business empire. The pattern of losing life in order to find it is not easily by-passed.

The other extreme form of contemporary self-understanding I want to use as a brief illustration is the post-modern or deconstructed self. In essence it could hardly be more different from the autonomous self, even though a protean character like Don Cupitt somehow manages to combine the two. In place of self-assertion, there is a denial that the self has any substantial reality at all. We float free, on a sea of transient influences and relationships. The search for truth or reality, beyond the reality of the passing moment, is a fool's errand, because the world we perceive has been shaped by our own way of speaking about it. Even sober scientific materialism is only one way of looking at the world among countless others, because all so-called knowledge is no more than interpretation, based on arbitrary choice. I am going to use a rather trivial example to illustrate it because, although post-modernism can claim some serious academic credentials, I feel increasingly that its real heartland is in the world of show business. In a recent interview, the actor Stephen Fry quoted Oscar Wilde as saying 'that those who live the artistic life can never know where they are going. The sole purpose of their lives is to realise themselves and find out who they are, whatever direction that might take.' Fry went on to say of himself, 'I don't want to be fixed in what I think. I'd like to believe that next year I'll believe nothing I say today, and everything I thought today I might think differently about.'4

Give or take a bit for the silly things people say when they are being interviewed, it is still by any standards a remarkable statement. If he meant it, he is implying no continuity between the self he is today and the self he might be tomorrow. If he didn't mean it, he is also implying no continuity between what he said yesterday and what he is saying today. Perhaps it is the influence of Oscar Wilde, whom he has just been playing. I find it interesting that, years before anybody invented post-modernism, G. K. Chesterton had put his finger on its essential emptiness in his critique of turn-of-the-century aestheticism, of which Wilde was a prime example.

Chesterton was writing in defence of rash vows, making the point that in committing ourselves, even to some foolish and extravagant undertaking, we are at least promising to meet ourselves at some future date, and to accept responsibility for what we are. 'To be everlastingly passing through dangers which we know cannot scathe us, to be taking oaths which we know cannot bind us, to be defying enemies who we know cannot conquer us – this is the grinning tyranny of decadence which is called freedom.' He went on to ridicule what Bernard Shaw had just then been writing on the subject of what he called 'free-love' – 'as if,' said Chesterton, 'a lover ever had been, or ever could be free. It is the nature of love to bind itself . . .'[5] His main point is a profoundly theological one, that human life is given its continuity and its dignity by our ability to be ourselves through time, to make promises and keep them.

This continuity need not preclude change, nor need it entail the 'bourgeoisification' which Fry describes as terrifying him – 'being fixed in a moral set of values and beliefs, and a set of people we do like and a set of people we don't like.'[6] There is a sense in which every life is a story in process of being written, a story of discovery and failure, a story which may take many twists and turns, but which progressively reveals what we truly are, and which is only complete when the last page is written. But without an acceptance that we ourselves, at whatever stage we are, have to own all of it, there can be no development of character, only one inconsequential change after another. We can only meaningfully become a different person, if we have come to terms with what we were before – if need be by what Christians call repentance. A person who lacks this awareness of continuity has been deconstructed in the most literal sense possible.

Let me now try to set what I have been saying more firmly in a theological context. The Bible is a story of promise and fulfilment. On the macro level the New Testament writers saw their gospel as fulfilling the scriptures then known to them. It was important to them that they could trace the continuity between the old Israel and the community of believers they had come to identify as the new Israel. There was a narrative theme running through history as they understood it, a narrative which had God as its author, and the final consummation of all things in Christ as its climax. Within this grand narrative there were countless lesser promises and fulfilments which marked God's continuing concern for his people. A prophet threatened judgement, and it happened. Another prophet promised restoration, and because people responded by acting in faith, that happened too. At the heart of the Christian message is the encouragement to hope against hope, because the impossible has happened in the Resurrection of Jesus Christ from the dead. The story, taken as a whole, is the story of God's self-giving love in coming to where his people are and remaining faithful to them.

It is a story which has been vigorously criticized at almost every level. It is true also that it can be, and has been, read in many different ways. Those who hold that God is a capricious tyrant who does indeed threaten human autonomy, have no lack of biblical texts. The Christian story can seem to others too narrowly exclusive to carry the universal claims made for it. And what about all those other religious stories which have sustained people's hopes and given meaning to their lives? Honest Christians have to admit that the picture is complex, that not all promises have been fulfilled, and that the mirrors in which we see ourselves remains dark, despite all our modern sophistication. Yet the story itself stubbornly resists being explained away or dismissed as irrelevant. Those who attend to it are still haunted by Christ's question, 'Who do you say that I am?' And Christians are not being disloyal if in answering that question they put it into a larger religious context. One of the great discoveries of inter-faith dialogue has been that, in spite of deep differences, one can find in other faiths echoes of the same themes of love as the basis of human relationships, faith as finding courage and continuity in the presence of God, grace as the empowerment which flows from this, and hope as that which gives meaning to our struggle to live worthwhile lives.

In this broad theological context, strong assertions of autonomy make no sense because all faiths, and Christian faith in particular, declare our inseparable relationships with one another, and hold that only in such relationship can we truly be ourselves. As regards post-modernism, only in Buddhism do we find the dissolution of the self as a goal, and it is no coincidence that Don Cupitt, now a prophet of religious post-modernism, has moved steadily in a Buddhist direction. But to lose the theme of promise and fulfilment is to miss precisely that sense of continuity which has given the Christian faith its energy. To lose the theme of self-discovery in the mirror of God's love for us, is to obscure the greatest possibilities of personal growth. To lose any awareness of, or openness towards, the God who wills to be along-side us, is to turn our backs on our best hope. In fact it is to bury Christ. But that has been done before – with unexpected results.

Notes

1. Anne Glyn-Jones, *Holding up a Mirror*, Century 1996, pp. 580– 581
2. Austin Farrer, *The Glass of Vision*, Dacre Press, 1948, p. 99
3. F. Nietzsche, *Thus Spake Zarathustra*, Everyman Edn. 1958, p. 76
4. Stephen Fry in the *Sunday Telegraph Magazine*, August 24th 1997
5. G. K. Chesterton, *Stories, Essays and Poems*, Everyman Edn. 1948, p. 117

Afterword

So who does interpret our society? Can we ever claim to have a clear and unbiased view of contemporary events? In attempting to see ourselves through the eyes of distinguished commentators, with specialist knowledge of their fields, have we cleared enough of the undergrowth of educational conditioning, parental influence and the economic and social factors which shape our world and our responses to it? Are we now in a position, to use a metaphor frequently used in these chapters, to hold a mirror to society and see ourselves clearly?

Sadly, I fear that we are not. Not only do we carry the inherited intellectual and emotional baggage of two thousand years of history; not only are we too close to events to have the historian's objective perspective, but this book has demonstrated that there are factors and ideologies which militate against such clarity.

In the first chapter, Libby Purves commented on our ability to create and to believe in 'instant social history': an instant social history purveyed by politicians and, to some extent, by the media. She then tellingly and amusingly described the distortions which skilled journalists can introduce into accounts of national and international affairs. The globalization of communication resulting from the spread of information technology worldwide leads not only to the homogenization of cultural distinctiveness, but also to an emphasis on speed of communication which can distort human response at an international level. Then she later points to the impact of 'spin doctors' and PR specialists who manipulate the news according to specific and independent agendas.

It was surely ever thus. But, when an itinerant peddler carried news from village to village, communication was a very slow process. Even after the invention of printing with moveable type in fifteenth-century Europe, knowledge and ideas were slow to spread and were confined to the literate. Nevertheless, Pope Innocent III was able to persuade vast areas of Western Christendom into the conviction that a 'Holy' war, a 'Just' war, against the infidel in Constantinople was a legitimate objective for contemporary society at the time. Indeed, he even managed to persuade the 'political' forces of the period that the eradication of non-conforming sects, such as the Cathars, was their duty. The distortion of facts, events and ideas involved in this exceptionally successful 'media' onslaught had a profound impact on the shape and nature of European society for centuries to come.

Let us focus upon another example, closer in time. During the eighteenth century, art and aesthetics were transferred from the realms of the sacred and spiritual to the secular. It was no longer necessary for the explicitly Christian iconography carved and painted in churches and cathedrals of the Romanesque and Gothic periods to be read as didactic. Instead it was invested with a moral and rational value which was disengaged from the subjective content. Art was becoming a substitute for religion, a means by which humanity could become free of day-to-day trivia and achieve spiritual enhancement and liberation through the contemplation of great art. From this view of art as an alternative to religious belief it was a very easy and, in some ways, logical step to equate art with education. Art, properly displayed and arranged, could be the handmaid of history and provide the onlooker with a coherent guide through time.

In 1835 Parliament set up a Select Committee to look into the management of art collections in public galleries and museums. The report, published in 1836, and the evidence given, especially by men such as the MP William Ewart (a member of the Committee), make fascinating reading. It is clear that the Committee was not only explicitly concerned with improving British economic competitiveness through better industrial design, in order to fight off challenges in our overseas markets from countries such as France, but also that its members held a positive view that art was socially valuable. Art embodied ideological potential which underpinned democracy and, by taking bold and innovative steps to articulate a belief in museums and art galleries, the 'temples of art', they were, in fact, controlling and manipulating the representation of history, science, art, and the natural and the social world to their fellow citizens. They were, it could be said, distorting truth to fit a political credo concerned with equality of access, self-improvement and the citizen's view of government in no less a thorough-going fashion than Innocent III. Thus, the average British citizen in the nineteenth century was as far from being able to see himself objectively as we are in the late twentieth century.

The view of the historian as an interpreter of contemporary society is rightly set in the context of the historian's traditional role of describing and explaining the past – to tell the 'story of the past' and to make it come alive. The responsibility of the historian is to be as objective an interpreter of primary and secondary source material as his or her conditioning by contemporary society will allow. Interpretation may be as orthodox or as controversial within his moral framework as the individual wishes. One can catalogue various eminent historians writing in the twentieth century whose views were, at first, regarded as controversial but whose writings have, in time, established a new orthodoxy. When Walter Ullmann began to publish his works on the history of the papacy in the 1940s, many ecclesiastical historians took issue with his fundamental emphasis on the papacy as exemplifying a complex unity of temporal and spiritual power in the Middle Ages. It would be a perverse historian, writing at the end of this century, who failed to take account of Ullmann's work. At the same time, however, that historian would need to correct the balance of opinion so forcefully expressed in works such as *The Growth of Papal Government in the Middle Ages* (1955).

The historian's ability to interpret the past has increasingly been assisted by the information technology which has developed over the past fifty years. In particular, economic historians have been able to interrogate vast data banks rapidly and draw conclusions which earlier would have taken many years to achieve. Different types of source material have become increasingly available which provide new means of interpreting the past. For example, oral history recordings, photographic and film archives, an increasing number of central government records such as Census returns, together with the extensive microfilming of parish registers, provide information not previously available. This has encouraged a shift of emphasis in the interpretation of history – away from the great constitutional and political issues to subjects such as the family and community, the place of women in society, and local and regional development. This new approach to traditional material has enabled us to see ourselves more clearly, but more clearly as part of an historical evolution. It has, however, not proved to be an aid towards illuminating the contemporary dilemma.

Lord Blake refers to the need for non-partisan histories of Ulster to balance the Protestant and Catholic bias of the material currently being taught in schools. The bias of religious interpretation has proved just as dangerously distorting in the past as was the political bias of Mao Tse-tung and Stalin. Society needs good historians with a deep sense of responsibility to their material and to their readers. A knowledge and insight into the past assists us in understanding the present – as Lord Blake describes it, 'the elucidation of historians' is required to develop an awareness of how certain problems were created, whether Ulster, Bosnia or the Welfare

State. However, what can never be assumed is that an understanding of the past will allow contemporary society to learn the lessons of history and 'see' the problems of the present with any greater insight.

For those whose working life will largely take place in the twenty-first century, the 'tools' by which they interpret their daily existence will almost certainly be information technology, which may be underpinned by a philosophical framework which could well owe much to the biological sciences. In the seventeenth century, scientists gained the confidence and certainty that the world was predictable, simple, and controllable through an inexorably logical explanation. This led to an intellectual excitement in the scientific community, partially explicable by the fact that they believed that they had the key to interpreting the physical world around them. This meant that understandings of the physical world and the moral world were equally open to logical dissection. We have heard from Dr Zohar that, in order to see ourselves, and to know and explain ourselves we need a new theory of ethics based on personal responsibility. This is a 'system' which will enable us to recognize that we can have a larger existence beyond ourselves. Dr Zohar has cogently advanced the view that ultimately everything will be related to scientific theory and principle, and that a 'physics of consciousness' will explain our higher aspirations. To achieve this new spiritual vision we require a sense of certainty based on an affirmed source of inspiration.

The question remains open. Can science provide this new source of vision and value? Our young biochemists and biotechnologists are among the most positive and optimistic members of our society, for they believe in their science. Do the rest of us, who are recipients of the benefits of science, have the same stalwart belief? My experience of contact with students over a period of some thirty years leads me to doubt the capacity of science alone to illuminate the ethical needs of our twentieth-century community. Familiarity and acceptance are no substitute for faith. We enter the year 2000 as a society in transition, but transition different in degree and direction from that which prefigured the approach to the second millennium. But we approach it to a different degree and from a different direction to the societal transition in the approach to the year 1000. Nevertheless, one certainty, which I believe we all now accept, is that society is evolutionary and organic, that it is ever changing.

Lord Habgood has stated that the 'freedom to be ourselves is fundamental to our humanity', but goes on to remark that 'two centuries of struggle to emancipate one group after another, have elevated autonomy to a primary goal'. He identifies two approaches to self-understanding in the process of attempting to see ourselves – the autonomous self and the deconstructed self – both of which he dismisses in favour of Christian repentance. A pre-condition of this repentance is that we must own our own human history, accepting both what we are and what we were before. This process can also be examined in the wider religious context of non-Christian faiths where, in some cases, love, grace and hope are also basic tenets governing human relationships.

At the close of the twentieth century, with the ending of the divisions in Europe described in Simpson's passage (quoted in the introduction to these lectures) and the discrediting of the dominant political ideologies which have shaped the world as we know it, we are left with an ideological vacuum, a vacuum which is unsatisfactorily filled at present by the prevailing emphasis on economic forces. To some, a return to fundamentalism (whether Islamic, Christian or Hindu) represents a way of giving meaning to that vacuum, of legitimizing our place in the world. This is achieved by adhering to a set of rigid values through which the we are enabled to interpret our contemporary society. It may temporarily feel safe, but it is a credo which will inevitably lead to bigotry in personal relations and confrontation in political terms. Religious fundamentalism all too easily becomes confused with cultural and national identity, and ultimately leads to a denial of individual human freedom and dignity.

This book, based on the first series of Launcelot Fleming lectures, has abundantly demonstrated the degree of uncertainty which reigns when different approaches to 'interpreting ourselves to ourselves' are probed by intelligent commentators. Recent radical changes in geopolitical alignments have destroyed our belief in a secure future. Environmental pollution, population explosion, depletion of food resources and natural disasters such as earthquake and famine, all contribute to a lack of confidence in ourselves as human beings. We are left with an unanswered question, a question which it is appropriate to pose and for which we must continue to demand an answer. My personal response is that the answer to this question must lie in continued inter-faith dialogue and multi-cultural experience. Only through an understanding of seemingly irreconcilable philosophies and approaches to religious belief will we learn the humility and tolerance with which to build new understanding and insight.

Elizabeth Estéve-Coll

VSE